What Peopl

*Embo*

Jenny Eades has written a lovely book in which she brings together the Franciscan spiritual tradition with the Alexander technique, showing how both can be integrated in a contemplative approach to living. It is evident that she walks the path of which she writes, and the result is a quiet wisdom and strength from which all who read or who meet her may draw. Her writing manifests simplicity, a right humility, joy and an 'at homeness' in the body as well as compassion and insight. It has been a healing process to read her words, and I am sure that many others will find it so too.
**Professor Nicola Slee**, author of *Praying Like a Woman* and *Sabbath: The hidden Heartbeat of Our Lives*

Jenny Fox Eades' Embodying Prayer is a gentle treasure that illuminates essential spiritual practices in a beautifully inclusive and accessible way. Eades centres the divinity of the body and reframes rest as fundamental to existence, both issues that are important to me as a Muslim disabled person dealing with chronic health challenges. I will be returning to the tender practices offered in each chapter. Skilfully weaving traditions, Embodying Prayer has given me a deeper appreciation and desire to experience more of the Alexander work, and reminded me of the blessings of dear St Clare and St Francis. Jenny Fox Eades is an important voice in the future of holistic worship that transcends religious dogma and self-imposed boundaries.
**Saimma Dyer**, Sufi facilitator and co-creator of RAY of God

Dr Fox Eades draws on her in depth experience of both the Alexander technique and The Third Order of St Francis to address the important but often neglected topic of integrating our awareness of our bodies with our spiritual lives.
**Revd Sue Walker,** TSSF

As a student of the Alexander Technique and a practicing Muslim of thirty years I find Jenny's confessional compassion rooted in her Christianity gives clarity to my own spiritual and elemental journey with Islam and the Alexander Technique. She answers so many questions for me.
**Chris (Abdul Kareem) Stone**

# Embodying Prayer

Exploring Franciscan Spirituality with
the Alexander Technique

# Embodying Prayer

Exploring Franciscan Spirituality with
the Alexander Technique

Jennifer M. Fox Eades

CHRISTIAN ALTERNATIVE
BOOKS

London, UK
Washington, DC, USA

# CollectiveInk

First published by Christian Alternative Books, 2024
Christian Alternative Books is an imprint of Collective Ink Ltd.,
Unit 11, Shepperton House, 89 Shepperton Road, London, N1 3DF
office@collectiveinkbooks.com
www.collectiveinkbooks.com
www.christian-alternative.com

For distributor details and how to order please visit the 'Ordering' section on our website.

ISBN: 978 1 80341 500 0
978 1 80341 501 7 (ebook)
Library of Congress Control Number: 2023908371

A CIP catalogue record for this book is available from the British Library.

Design: Lapiz Digital Services

UK: Printed and bound by CPI Group (UK) Ltd, Croydon, CR0 4YY
Printed in North America by CPI GPS partners

We operate a distinctive and ethical publishing philosophy in all areas of our business, from our global network of authors to production and worldwide distribution.

This book is dedicated to my Union Chapel Alexander groups.
Thank you for all you have given me.

# Contents

Preface                                                               1

Foreword                                                              4

Acknowledgements                                                      6

Chapter 1   St Francis, St Clare and F M Alexander        7
  Embodied Prayer Practice: Go for a Walk                 16

Chapter 2   Help Me to Live                               17
  Embodied Prayer Practice: Refrain from Speaking         26
  Embodied Prayer Practice: Coming to Quiet               27

Chapter 3   Help Me to Lean                               28
  Embodied Prayer Practice: Rest                          38
  Embodied Prayer Practice: Stand Firm                    39

Chapter 4   Help Me to Meet Others                        40
  Embodied Prayer Practice: Opening                       51
  Embodied Prayer Practice: Reading a Poem Aloud          52

Chapter 5   Help Me to Wait                               54
  Embodied Prayer Practice: The Soft Gaze                 66
  Embodied Prayer Practice: Kneeling to Pray              67

Chapter 6   Help Me to Look Forward to Tomorrow           69
  Embodied Prayer Practice: Singing a Psalm               77

Chapter 7   Befriending Ourselves                         79
  Embodied Prayer Practice: Centering Prayer              88

Chapter 8—Final Words from Clare and Francis              90

Author Biography                           91
Previous Titles                            92
References                                 93
Further Reading                           100
Glossary of Terms                         101

# Preface

In 2014 I qualified, after four years and 1,600 hours of training, as a teacher of the Alexander technique. Alexander is a 100 year old, Western self-help technique that is best known as a way of helping bad backs. It is a movement-based, contemplative body/ mind discipline, and what always interested me most about it was that practising it felt very like meditation. In Alexander work you learn to be quiet at a deep, physical and emotional level. You learn to be more aware of your whole self, body, mind and spirit and of your environment.

In 2015 I made a lifelong commitment as a member of the Third Order of the Society of St Francis. The Third Order are not monks or nuns but lay people who try to walk the Christian spiritual pathway with a particular focus on the virtues of love, simplicity and justice, inspired by the life and teachings of St Francis and St Clare of Assisi.

This book is a series of reflections on how these two spiritual paths—and I do see the Alexander technique as a spiritual path though not all Alexander teachers would agree with me—intertwine.

Some people use the Alexander technique to play the violin or to sing more easily. Others learn it to run without injury. Many people come to it to find relief from chronic pain. It is a technique or a practice, that helps you to do the things you do with ease and grace and pleasure. I use it to practice my religion, to pray, to walk along the path of Christ in the footsteps of Francis and Clare.

So, this is not a book about the Alexander technique per se. There are plenty of excellent Alexander books by teachers with far more experience than I. Nor is it a book about following St Francis and St Clare—I am not an expert and leave that to others. This book is about how I draw on the example and teachings of Francis, Clare and F.M. Alexander to pray and to live out my vocation of being loved in the world.

The philosopher John Dewey said that it is of grace not of ourselves that we lead civilised lives.[1] To put it another way, as one of our Third Order principles puts it, we have nothing that we have not first received.[2] It is therefore our duty — and our privilege and our joy — to offer what we can and what we have received in the hope that it will be of use to others. It is in this spirit that I offer these reflections.

# Use of Terms

There is an increasing tendency in modern writing to drop the hyphen in 'well-being' so that it becomes wellbeing. I prefer to keep it because I don't think being well is a noun, a thing inside us that we can measure easily. It is more of an adverb, do we live well or in a way that makes us unwell?

I also follow some feminist theologians in mostly preferring to use the term 'kin-dom' rather than kingdom of heaven. It is a way of emphasising the fundamental importance of relationship to all social and spiritual experiences, and a gentle push against the dominance of masculine and hierarchical language and imagery.

# Foreword

In a simple, unassuming way, this book points us towards doorways into new and profound experiences. Jenny Fox Eades shares her honest reflections about her journey of self-discovery, identifying signposts along the way that are relevant to helping each of us on our journey.

At first, it may seem odd that a follower of St Francis and St Clare should write about the joy of having the Alexander technique—better known for alleviating aches and pains—as a tool and companion for her spiritual journey. However, freeing ourselves from the constraints of habit, and placing trust in some greater guiding power, is necessary for both.

Jenny points out that Western Christianity has long regarded mind and body as separate entities, ignoring the body and giving priority to the reasoning intellect. In general, we now have a greater understanding of the interdependence of all our faculties and how our physicality is the means for connecting with other aspects of living. The Alexander technique makes no claim as a spiritual discipline, yet, as the Anglican Fr Geoffrey Curtis observed, by applying its simple principles, one is disciplined spiritually through the self-realisation that can arise. It provides the educational bridge between idealistic theory and what it is possible to do—or choose *not to do*—in practice.

Today, it is all too easy to get swept along in the tide of competing demands for our attention. We can feel unsure about doing anything that might make a difference; at the same time, we fear change and the unknown. It seems that to give ourselves time and permission to stop and to appreciate the sky above, the ground beneath and the air we breathe—is as good a place as anywhere to start any journey afresh and to discover what happens next.

In keeping with this ethos, Jenny concludes each section with some simple practices—starting from here-now and doing what is practical. As is often remarked, these are simple though not necessarily easy; but their effectiveness is in their simplicity. So be patient, be persistent, be kind to yourself and keep an open, lively interest, and—most of all—be trusting.

Malcolm Williamson

Former Head of Training at Manchester Alexander Technique Training School

Edinburgh, April 2022

# Acknowledgements

Any book builds on the gifts, the teaching, and the sheer undeserved help given by so many people. I want to highlight the debt I owe to the writings of Richard Rohr, who speaks the truths of the Christian faith in words I can relate to; to my Franciscan colleagues who travel with me and especially Debby Plummer, for cheerful, hopeful companionship; to my Alexander teachers, Malcolm Williamson, Liz Hulse, Peter Bloch, Bruce Fertman and the many colleagues and teachers and students I continue to learn from and with; to Malcolm Williamson, again, for helpful edits and suggestions that add to clarity about Alexander terms; to Professor Herbert Richardson for suggesting I write this book in the first place; to Brother Hugh SSF for always going to Greenbelt and being a great advert for all things Franciscan; to the Greenbelt Festival for existing and keeping hope alive; to those I worship and pray with and have worshiped and prayed with, past and present; to Richard Carter for permission to use his poem; to St Martins-in-the-Fields for being a deep spiritual resource for me and many others during Covid; to Nick, for editing and reading every word numerous times and for being my companion and friend and dearest love, in all things.

The poem 'Joy' by Richard Carter, from *In Search of the Lost* is used with permission of the author and of the publisher, Canterbury Press.

# Chapter 1

# St Francis, St Clare and F M Alexander

## Spiritual Pathways

In 2010 I started on two distinct paths. One path was that of becoming an Alexander technique teacher. The other was becoming a member of the Anglican religious order, The Third Order of the Society of St Francis. At that time, I saw no great connection between these two strands of my life. One was professional, the other spiritual. Over the years, as I have studied the Alexander technique and explored what it means to attempt to follow in the way of Christ after the example of St Francis and St Clare, I have come to see that the two strands have entwined with one another to the extent that I now see my Alexander work as embodying my Franciscan Christian principles and my Franciscan Christian principles as the heart and soul of my Alexander work.

In this book, I use a prayer by St Francis to explore how I have come to understand Alexander work, in my own experience, as an embodied, contemplative discipline. I reflect on how I use it, moment by moment, to be more aware of myself in my environment and to be more aware of the Real, which is another way of referring to God. Each line of the prayer forms the subject and title of a separate chapter. This is the prayer:

Help me to live this day quietly, easily.
Help me to lean on thy great strength trustfully, restfully.
Help me to meet others joyously, peacefully.
Help me to wait for the unfolding of thy will patiently,
    serenely.
Help me to look forward to tomorrow confidently, courageously.

In a final chapter, I explore how I practice 'Centering Prayer', as taught by Cynthia Bourgeault, and draw together my reflections in light of that central practice.

One paradox (there are many in both Christianity and Alexander work) is that Francis never wrote a book and thoroughly disapproved of them. Another is that the Alexander technique is a felt experience, more or less impossible to convey in words. However, I was first asked to write this book by someone who was passionately interested in *both* Francis *and* the Alexander technique, so I offer it in the hope that it *will* somehow be of use in the wider scheme of things. What other reason is there to write anything? So, I will ask St Francis to forgive me for adding to the number of books in the world and F M Alexander to forgive my mangled attempts to put his life's work and insight into words.

## Three Outsiders

The Third Order of the Society of St Francis is part of a wider, worldwide Franciscan movement. There are Franciscans in different Christian denominations all around the world. The Third Order, of which I am a member, is part of the Church of England. First Order Franciscans are monks and nuns who, like Francis, combine the life of work and prayer. The Second Order are contemplatives, prayer *is* their work. They follow the pattern of St Clare, Francis' close friend and early follower, and they are sometimes called Poor Clares, after their commitment to poverty. The Third Order was first founded by St Francis himself. A village wanted to follow him but had families to feed and work to do. So, St Francis created a rule that would allow them to live simply, after his example, but without becoming monks or nuns.

In the 20th century, the Third Order was re-founded within the Anglican Church. It is called TSSF or The Third Order of the Society of St Francis and its members are sometimes called tertiaries. We wear no distinguishing clothing, we may be lay or ordained, married or single but we all promise to follow a rule of life, which we design for ourselves, with guidance from others. And we make a commitment to live simply, to work for social justice and to share the love of God.

I joined the Third Order—or rather I began the three-year process of exploring *whether* to join the Order—when I became aware of a desire for 'something more' in my spiritual journey. And I knew about the Franciscans because they were a regular feature at the Greenbelt Festival of Faith and Arts that my family attend each year.

I began training as an Alexander technique teacher because the technique intrigued me. I was aware that it changed me, calmed me, and the training school I visited in Manchester was unlike any educational institution I had ever encountered. I wanted to know more. In both cases, I did not know what I was joining. They were unknown pathways into unfamiliar territory. I felt something calling me down that particular path.

St Francis' joyful, playful, gentle spirituality, his love and care for the world around him, and his deep love for all people and all things is still compelling today. One of the reasons I chose a Franciscan order to join was that Francis, like his master, took women seriously. When Francis needed advice, he turned to St Clare. Her presence and teachings within the Franciscan tradition help integrate the feminine with the masculine and, for me, go a little way toward balancing the overwhelmingly masculine legacy of Christianity.

I was also struck by the cheerfulness of the Franciscans I knew. They loved deeply and did not appear to take themselves too seriously. There was a twinkle in their eye that I found attractive. And one of the things I liked most about the founder of the Alexander technique (who was definitely no saint) was a comment he made that one should go through life with a twinkle in the eye, not taking oneself too seriously.

Francis, Clare and Alexander were all, it seems to me, outsiders. F M Alexander was a maverick who invented a mind/body discipline that is difficult to put into words. He was just outside the edge of the medical system, as the Alexander technique still is today. St Francis and St Clare were always right on the edge of the institutional church, though just on the inside, rather than just outside it. Francis, Clare and Alexander all taught others how to do things differently, and how to *be* different in the world. They paid attention to different things and focused on *how* we act as well as what we do. They did not engage in head-on conflict with accepted practices but worked indirectly and around the edges of systems and behaviours. They were all counter-cultural individuals. They worked through actions and their embodied selves, through *how* they were in the world, far more than through words. I have always felt myself to be something of an outsider and counter-cultural, albeit in a quiet kind of way. So, I was perhaps ready and happy to journey with these outsiders and to learn from them how to *be* different in the world.

## Seeing What Is Really There

The Alexander technique has been described as a movement-based, contemplative embodied practice.[3] This seems appropriate since the Alexander technique is about seeing what is really there and that, for me, is also the essence of contemplation. One of Alexander's key principles is that our senses are not always reliable. We come to rely on the usual ways we sit, stand, move, and hold ourselves, our usual patterns of movement, tension, thinking and behaviour. These are developed and practised over many years, often without change. We may, for example, think that we are standing straight or that our feet are parallel. But what we are doing is standing the way that we usually stand, with our feet where we usually place them. What we feel is simply familiarity, and a mirror may reveal something quite different. In studying Alexander work we learn to see ourselves more clearly, and to develop a more or less constant awareness of the embodied self within its environment. We learn to maintain an awareness of both the self *and* the environment, rather than either/or. Usually, we focus either on the mountain we are climbing, the screen we are typing on, *or* on our feet, fingers or back, but not usually on both at the same time.

Contemplation also changes how we see. It is looking with appreciation, with a recognition of the beauty and the wonder of what we behold. Seeing what is really there. Seeing reality. Contemplation has been called a long-loving look at the real.[4] And it can be a way of developing a more or less constant awareness of the connectedness between everything, including our own connection with our environment.

Richard Rohr says of spiritual giants like St Francis and St Clare that they occupy liminal space, a space in between states or roles, on the edge or periphery of the dominant culture. In such liminal, marginal states or places, they see differently and are constantly open to the new, the unexpected. They remain, always empty and receptive. When he speaks of liminal space as a place where we need to not-do and not perform according to our usual successful patterns,[5] he could be quoting from a book on the Alexander technique.

My study of the technique, which is constant, day by day, and moment by moment, helps me to perceive when I am on autopilot, when I am following my habits or patterns of self-defence, self-protection and self-promotion. It helps me 'not-do and not perform' according to my usual patterns. It doesn't *ensure* that I don't follow them. But it does give me a little more space in which I can pause and notice what I am doing or about to do and perhaps choose *not* to do it. So, for me, the Alexander technique is a practical, physical tool for learning to walk a spiritual path of dying to self and opening to the other, to the Divine, to Reality, to the newness in each moment, step by step, breath by breath.

## Bodies and Beyond

F M Alexander, working in the early years of the 20th century, was a man ahead of his time in questioning the dominant, Western idea of a split between mind and body. This idea pervades both Western philosophy and religion. Early Greek philosophers, such as Plato, condemned the body as inferior and at best a servant to, at worst a distraction from, the all-important life of the mind.[6] Descartes is credited with contributing to what we now call dualism, the split of body and mind into two distinct spheres.

In Christianity, the words of St Paul are often interpreted as implying that true Christian living can only be achieved by subjugating the body.[7] While there are scholars who argue for a much more positive reading of St Paul, his writings and those of other Christian thinkers have contributed to a deep unease with the physical that is still problematic within Christianity, and indeed beyond. Cynthia Bourgeault says that in many spiritual traditions, the body is viewed with fear and suspicion as the 'seat of desire and at best a dumb beast that must be trained and brought into submission to the personal will'.[8]

Yet at the same time, all religious traditions have insisted that religious life cannot be practised with the mind alone. I find it fascinating that the Jewish scriptures contain numerous references to the Israelites having stiff necks. For example, in Exodus 32:9, God says to Moses: 'I have seen this people, how stiff-necked they are'. I am fascinated because, as an Alexander technique teacher, at its simplest level I am helping people to unstiffen their necks! A stiff neck not only causes pain but reduces our ability to sense and respond to the rest of ourselves and to the world around us. A stiff neck is a physical *and* a spiritual issue.

When we look at Christianity, we find that the resurrection of the body is a central, albeit profoundly mysterious, Christian idea. The stories of Christ's resurrection appearances are deeply physical. Thomas puts his hands into Christ's wounds, and Jesus barbecues fish for his followers on the beach. He breaks bread with them. Christ left his followers a very physical metaphor and ritual, 'this is my body, this is my blood' around which the church has built much of its spiritual life. And yet we persistently undervalue the physical, the material. As Bruce Fertman, one of my teachers says, 'We've created a disembodied concept of soul, disconnected from the biological world, and have separated matter from spirit. This means that matter is without soul and unholy, and can therefore be exploited, abused, and discarded'.[9]

The terms 'soma/somatic' have come to refer to the thinking, living, feeling, sensing body, as opposed to a physical body devoid of thought. They are used to refer to a range of disciplines including Tai Chi and the Alexander technique that seek to transcend the body/mind dualism that is so pervasive in Western thought and language. In such somatic disciplines, the aim is to experience the body from within, in such a way that the body and mind are not separated but are experienced as a whole.[10]

St Francis was an important figure in bringing the physical humanity of Christ to the fore in Christian thought, in developing a sense of the soul within matter, of the goodness within creation and, also, of our inter-relatedness with God, with one another, with Brother Sun, Sister Moon and Mother Earth. The whole thrust of Franciscan theology is a focus on Christ's very real human suffering and the Incarnation of God, the Divine, present in human bodies, present in, and in love with, the whole of material creation.

My training as an Alexander teacher taught me to teach with my hands and to use my whole physically embodied self to help others feel more comfort and less discomfort, more at home, more free within their own physical, emotional and spiritual selves. I see my Alexander work and my Franciscan vocation as engaged in a continuous conversation, one that hopefully makes me a better Alexander teacher and a more incarnational Franciscan. My hope is that as I increase my knowledge of myself, I increase in understanding and compassion for others.[11]

## Beyond Language

A final point of connection I find between my paths of Alexander work and being a follower of St Francis and St Clare is that both present a challenge to language and understanding, because both go far beyond the verbal in what they encompass. The Alexander technique is notoriously difficult to describe. It is an experience of freedom, a self-help technique that requires a teacher, an 'embodied movement discipline', a 'body/mind practice', a 'somatic discipline'. There are no exercises in it. It is about how we do *everything* we do, about how we *are* in the world. It always has been, and remains, difficult to grasp, to write about and indeed to practise. It places demands on the individual, to practise awareness, to notice oneself, to see what is there, to risk change and willingly grow beyond what might be familiar or comfortable, to step into liminal space and not grasp at certainty, not rush into the future.

In an introduction to Alexander's book *Constructive Conscious Control of the Individual*, John Dewey asks whether the Alexander technique was cheap and easy, or whether it made demands on the intellectual and moral energies of the individuals concerned.[12] Alexander work is simple, certainly. But it is not easy, nor cheap and it makes huge intellectual and moral demands. It is a very real practice with very real effects. But it is hard to put into words because words can never fully convey what is essentially a feeling or experience. Likewise, the stuff of religion, prayer, spirit, and God—these are beyond language and, in the case of the Divine, beyond human understanding by definition. As St Augustine said, what is grasped quickly is insufficiently valued.[13]

However, in our modern age of fast food and fast information, there is a tendency to only value 'what is grasped quickly'. The disciplines of religion and somatic practices like the Alexander technique are rejected by many as too esoteric, too impractical, and perhaps even too difficult. They cannot be measured or valued in monetary terms, and hence in our money and measurement-obsessed age, they can be seen as somehow meaningless. They are both, to quote the title of Scott Peck's famous book, roads less travelled.[14] For me, that is where the excitement lies!

# Embodied Prayer Practice: Go for a Walk

A saying attributed to St Francis is that it is no use walking anywhere to preach unless our walking *is* our preaching.[15]

My interpretation of this is that each step we take, each breath we breathe is as much a communication of the love of God as the words that we say. We can walk mindlessly, aggressively, ruminating on the past, anxious for the future. Or we can walk 'to exercise', grimly determined to get to the end of our allotted distance, sweaty and out of breath, with calories burned and muscles moved. In either case, a channel through which the world can see and hear the love of God, which is the human being, consciously serving the Divine, is a touch muddy and a little bit blocked.

A walk that is lovingly alive to the present moment, thankfully aware of the feel of the ground beneath our feet, joyfully conscious of the privilege and pleasure of being an embodied, fleshy, created child of God, is a sermon in and of itself.

So, go for a walk and listen to your footsteps and the birds. Leave the headphones behind, along with your worries! And listen to the sound of your breathing. Think about how you walk. Don't worry about what you look like. Enjoy your moving, fleshy self. Don't try to directly change how you walk, but think about the earth on which you walk as sacred, as your Mother Earth's body. Walk with thoughts of being open to the love of God, or to the love of Mother Earth, or just 'openness' and 'lightness', if you prefer. Be thankful, that you can walk as not everyone can. It is a gift.

And then notice what you notice. Do these thoughts make a difference to *how* you walk and to your embodied experience of walking?

# Chapter 2

# Help Me to Live

## Quiet Outside and Quiet Inside

Alexander work has been called a way of exploring quietness.[16] I was taught that Alexander sometimes referred to his work as 'coming to quiet', which is a phrase I have grown to love. Usually, our minds are full of chatter, our bodies full of tension, of getting ready to do all sorts of things which our minds are already anticipating. It seems surprisingly difficult for humans, with their imaginations and fears and goals for the future, and their memories of the past, to be present in, and attentive to, the here and now.

In recent years it seems as if we have become ever busier, and ever more tense. In the past, leisure was a sign of high status. These days, being constantly on the go, working hard and playing hard, is seen as the ideal. Important people have little time, now, for leisure. Being 'time-poor' is a mark of high status. The highly successful don't take holidays, they take 'mini breaks'. Not being busy or having nothing to do is variously seen as a mark of failure or inadequacy. For some, it seems frightening and is a state they avoid at all costs. At the same time, being time-poor is also a mark of poverty, since we often pay low-status work so badly that people engaged in it need multiple jobs just to earn enough to feed themselves and their families.

Notice also how our goals have changed. We no longer go for a daily walk to stretch our legs and enjoy the fresh air. No, now we go for runs 'to keep fit', not pausing to ask ourselves, 'fit for what?' And it is no longer enough to just go for runs. Now we must run marathons, or multiple marathons or iron man challenges. Of course, many people do no such thing. They watch television or browse social media to excess instead. But these extremes of physical exercise are held up to us as ideals.

One of my observations of families during the period of Covid 19 lockdown was that, with so many other activities cancelled, people were learning to go for walks again. And children, with no school taking up long hours, followed by multiple after-school activities, followed by homework, were learning how to play. They were walking around and noticing what was in the windows of the houses they walked past or playing hopscotch. It was, quite literally, quieter outside as traffic and aeroplanes gave way to bird song.

As students of Alexander work, we are taught to notice, physically, when we are not quiet. Often, we hold much more muscular tension in our bodies than we need for any action. We stride, ramming our feet down on the ground and pushing our thigh bones into our hip joints. We grip our coffee mugs or pencils, twisting our fingers, distorting our hands. We jab at our keyboards as if they were old-fashioned typewriters, requiring immense effort to push down each key, instead of the lightest of taps.

All this effort and tension is, quite literally, noisy. If you walk with less force, your footfalls will be quieter. If you type with less effort you will make less sound on the keyboard. Learning to first notice when I use more effort than is needed, and then to turn down the volume control on that effort so that it is quieter, both in muscular and decibel terms is part of what Alexander work helps me to do.

## Quiet Enough to Listen

As an Alexander teacher, quietening down my responses, my musculature, my inner dialogue, helps me, in turn, to listen to others. I listen with my ears to what my students say and how they say it. I listen with my hands to the tensions in their bodies, to the very physical stories that bodies tell about the life that has been lived in them. It is one reason that teaching Alexander work is such a joy. I find refreshment in my habits of thought and behaviour when I teach, and I benefit from listening to the lived embodied wisdom of the person I am teaching. And when I am quiet enough to listen, really listen, to myself, to my student, to my environment, I make it easier for the still small voice of the Divine to make itself heard too.

Quietness, living quietly, has both a physical and a spiritual quality to it. Richard Rohr notes that in terms of spirituality, as in good art, less is usually more.[17] Much of what we do, much of what I do, is a way of keeping busy, of creating so much physical and emotional 'noise', of distracting myself from the harder task of being human, of being fully aware and fully alive. I can waste my time on social media, I can fritter my attention and energy on watching television. The Alexander technique can help me notice when I am doing that and instead choose to be quiet, to listen and to be still, paying attention to what IS, to reality, in the here and the now. In all honesty, I must add that I often don't succeed at this. Frequently I succumb to distracting myself, absenting myself, and filling my mind with chatter. But occasionally, just occasionally, quietness and presence prevail.

## Moving Easily

One of my favourite words when teaching the Alexander technique is 'ease'. I aim to teach people to move and to live more easily, more gently, with less effort, less strain, and less tension. So 'living the day easily' can and does refer to the physical quality of my movement. Can I be more aware of my movements and their quality? Can I make my physical movements easier, gentler? And if I can manage to make my physical movement easier, gentler, less strained, less jerky, and less sudden, then that will have an emotional effect, a psychological effect, and a spiritual effect too. Because we are psychophysical, emotional and spiritual creatures.

So, I can apply the word 'ease' to how I respond to my physical environment, to how I hold a cup or tap a keyboard. And I can also apply it to how I respond to what happens around me, to what is said to me, to what I read on social media or hear on the radio. Do I fly off the handle, get swamped by anxiety, and feel irritated or threatened when others think differently from me? Can I 'live easily' and allow others to be what they are, which is different from me? Can I allow circumstances to be what they are, which is never perfect? Can I see and accept reality for what it IS, rather than demanding that it be different to suit me?

That does not necessarily mean not seeking to change circumstances if that is what I am given to do. Part of my Franciscan commitment, after all, is a promise to fight against all injustice.[18] But it might mean trying to do that, too, easily. Richard Rohr says that St Francis and St Clare always avoided head-on conflict. Instead, they critiqued the bad at the heart of institutions by the practice of the good on the edges of that institution. The best criticism of the bad is the practice of the better.[19] So, if I see something I think is unjust, I ask myself if I can critique and challenge it gently, by stepping to one side and practising differently.

Above all, can I still see the humanity of those I disagree with and who disagree with me? Can I continue to see each person, however wrong their actions may be in my view, as a child of God and therefore as my sister or brother? Sadly, the answer to that question is so often 'No I can't'. I have habits of defensiveness, habits of fear and anger that are deep-seated. However, what my practice of self-awareness does help me to do — and the Alexander technique and being Franciscan are both paths of self-awareness — is to catch myself falling into those habits. Self-awareness helps me notice that I am *not* living today easily, not seeing the humanity in each person. And it helps me to at least *try* and stop doing what Alexander called 'the wrong thing', which is the first step toward change and allowing the 'right' thing to happen in me.

Because it is only when I have stopped ranting, stressing or defending myself that Providence can have a chance of working in and through me.

## Being Easy with Imperfection

One ingrained habit I have become much more aware of in myself in recent years is perfectionism. And sadly, judging myself harshly, and a tendency to judge others, too, goes hand in hand with that perfectionism. So, being me can be quite hard work! Bruce Fertman teaches that Alexander teachers need to see themselves and others accurately *and* benevolently.[20] Now, how I see myself and how I see others are linked. If I judge *myself* harshly that will make me more likely to judge others harshly. If I get angry with myself for not being perfect, I will tend to be angry with others for not being perfect too. Conversely, I cannot see others benevolently if I cannot see myself benevolently.

And seeing benevolently and seeing accurately are also linked. Blind optimism isn't benevolent, seeing myself or others through rose-tinted spectacles isn't benevolent. Real benevolence, real loving kindness sees the truth, and it is the truth that sets us free. If we are out of touch with reality, says Martin Laird, then we are out of touch with ourselves, with others and with God.[21] And the truth is, the reality is, that I am not perfect, and neither is anybody else. It is possible to interpret Alexander himself as aiming for the 'perfection' of humankind. Personally, I see the tendency to want perfection as being part of the 'shadow side' of the Alexander technique and it is not how I seek to practise it. I use it not to become perfect, which is impossible, but to stop *trying* to be perfect.

Unfortunately, Christianity has contributed to a harshness towards our physical selves within our culture. The body is somehow distanced from 'me' and needs to be made fitter, stronger, thinner, than it currently is. Increasingly we eat or don't eat certain foods for 'health' and forget about the human need for pleasure. We don't move because we enjoy movement, we 'exercise' in order to get 'fit'. And people believe the 'no pain no gain' mantra of the fitness industry and push through tiredness, pain and discomfort as though they are signs of weakness to be overcome rather than bodily wisdom trying to get through to us. Ignoring one's body in this way is rarely, if ever, a good idea, on any level. Being harder, faster, longer, and thinner is not always better. Aiming for perfection might benefit the fitness and diet industries but it doesn't benefit real human beings.

The truth is that bodies are fragile and imperfect; they get tired, they can be damaged, they age and eventually die. Accepting that isn't defeatist, it is just true. At the same time, it is also true that I am not helpless in the face of ageing and ill health. There are simple things I can do to help myself be well, rather than perfect. I can influence my body, take care of myself and help myself be a little fitter, a little healthier, and a little easier in my embodied self, whatever my current state of health or ill health.

So, yes, I exercise, though at least as much for pleasure and as prayer as for 'health'. And I eat what I love, though in moderation. And when I set out for a run and I realize I'm tired, I walk. And when I have been standing for a while and my legs ache, I sit. And when I eat a little more than I need I try to inhibit my habit of beating myself up for it. And when I ache somewhere I try to let go of judging myself for being less supple than I might be or feeling the need to fix myself. So, I apply the Alexander technique by first accepting that this is where and how I am at present. Then I try to be gentle and caring towards myself, and curious about what is happening.

My Franciscan path also helps me subvert my tendency towards perfectionism. St Francis said that we can show love to others by not wishing that they should be better than they are;[22] thus, Franciscan spirituality is a spirituality of imperfection.[23] A willingness to love and cheerfully accept that I, and everyone else for that matter, is imperfect.

I can show love for myself by accepting that I am not perfect and never will be. And I can show love for my Alexander students by *not* wishing to fix them or needing them to be other than they truly are. Yes, I want them to be more comfortable if they are uncomfortable. I want them to feel more at ease if they feel too tense. I want them, basically and fundamentally, to enjoy their gorgeous miraculous embodied selves in all their complexity, beauty and imperfection as much as they can, and to get to know and appreciate themselves more. I see my role as helping that to happen.

## Speaking Easily

I can also apply the idea of living 'easily' today to what I say. Speech is a physical act, with all the overtones of emotion and psyche that accompany each physical act. And it is a spiritual act, too. Learning to be conscious of what we say and how we say it is an important part of many spiritual traditions. Buddhists have the concept of 'right speech'. This is traditionally presented within Buddhism as abstaining from wrong speech, from idle chatter, from hurtful words and lies. For me, this echoes Alexander's idea of first needing to stop doing the 'wrong' thing. Positively, Buddhism teaches that one should say only what is true and beneficial, what is motivated by kindness. Jesus also warns against the lies and slander that defile us, against saying things that create barriers between people, or between people and God. What we say and how we say it matters.

Christian monastic orders consider the training of speech to be an important part of the spiritual life. St Clare of Assisi laid down guidelines for the sisters of her order that they should say only what is really necessary, quietly and briefly.[24] Likewise, St

Augustine thought it was better to keep silent than to speak and that one should only speak if absolutely necessary. Christians, he said, should want to listen, not to speak.[25]

Interestingly, the Alexander technique began when F M Alexander lost his ability to speak during acting performances. His understanding of how to prevent himself from tensing his body unnecessarily when on the stage forms the basis for what we now know as Alexander work. In its early years, it was very much known as a breathing and speech discipline. So, I can certainly apply Alexander principles to how I speak and breathe, but, importantly, I can also apply them to *what* I say, and when and how I say it.

For example, gradually, over the course of my training, I began to notice how, in a group situation, I felt a certain compulsion to 'chip in' to conversations when they were about subjects of interest to me. I seemed to need to show how much I knew. And, even more gradually, it has dawned on me that the habits I have around my behaviour in groups are precisely that: habits or patterns of feeling and behaving, formed over many years of being in human groups, starting with my own family, the very first group I experienced. I, therefore, began to try, and I still try, to remember that I don't *have* to say something in every conversation, I don't have to have my moment in the spotlight or show what I know and what I think.

Of course, others, in groups, may have the reverse habit. Their habit may be of never speaking, never contributing to the conversation. In effect, they habitually *withhold* their contribution from the group. There is nothing inherently wrong with either speaking or not speaking, provided that what we say is constructive or that our silence in a conversation is motivated by kindness and compassion.

Alexander work helps me to notice my habits and indeed my motivation. To be 'easy' is not to feel compelled, to be free to opt for speech or silence. And we may be 'compelled' by unconscious habit or by past practices and events, as much as by present circumstances. Part of the reason Alexander work can feel very liberating is that it slowly lays bare and undoes unconscious habits, thus providing us with more freedom in the present, in thought, in movement and speech.

This allows me to choose whether to speak, and when I do speak, to make sure that what I say is helpful, kind or generous. I am free to speak. I am free to be silent. It is also important that those of us with more freedom to speak in our society, with more voice, use that voice to create space and opportunity for the relatively voiceless. I have more voice than others because I am an adult, white, educated and relatively wealthy. I have less voice than others because I am female and come from a working class background. Part of the Franciscan call is to help create a society in which all are equally free to speak or to be silent. That is what we call the Kingdom of Heaven, or as I prefer, the Kin-dom of Heaven.

# Embodied Prayer Practice:
# Refrain from Speaking

In a group situation, notice your habits. Do you dominate conversations, interrupt, need to win arguments or show people how erudite you are? If so, see if you can refrain, on occasion, from one of those habits. Conversely, if you are somebody who habitually does *not* speak up in group situations, notice that. You have a contribution to make that the group may need to hear. Try speaking and see what happens.

# Embodied Prayer Practice: Coming to Quiet

This practice is the closest that the Alexander technique has to an exercise, and it is described and recommended in most books on the Alexander technique. It is called different things: 'semi-supine', 'active rest' or 'lying down work'. My preferred term for it is 'Coming to Quiet'. I see it as a form of prayer though, of course, many other teachers would see it differently. We encourage students to practise it daily as it has many benefits, not least a growth in being able to be quiet. It is also, quite pragmatically, the best thing you can do either for a painful back or to keep your back in good shape!

Find a warm, quiet place in your home with enough space to lie down on the floor. Put a rug or mat beneath you and gather two or three books or a firm cushion to go under your head. Take your time and gently lie down on the mat with your head supported and your knees flexed and pointing at the ceiling (this puts less strain on your back than lying with your legs straight out).

Let your hands rest on your body and have your feet in line with your hips. Keep your eyes open and pay gentle attention to your body and your environment. Notice if you are tense in some areas and show those areas kindness and permission to be less tense. Smiling lets your facial muscles relax and encourages ease in the rest of the body. Imagine a smile across your chest, between your shoulder blades, and across the tops of your knees. Imagined smiles encourage ease and expansion in our muscles.

Let the floor support you. Notice the gentle rise and fall of your breath. You are safe. There is nowhere to go and nothing to do. Stay here for 5 or 10 minutes, or longer if you wish. This is a pause in your day to be quiet, to be easy, to care for yourself so that you can more easily care for others and our world.

# Chapter 3

# Help Me to Lean

## Trusting the Ground

I have come to love the moment, first thing in the morning, when I stand in front of my open window and ask the Divine to help me to *lean* on her great strength — trustfully, restfully. It is when I remind myself that I can trust the ground beneath my feet, that I can 'give my feet to the ground', that the ground — and God — are simply there and I don't have to hold myself up, don't have to achieve anything to be acceptable to the Divine, don't have to try so hard. The ground and God and Love are simply *there*, to lean on, to help me through — to trust. So, I can do less.

And I remember that I have heels as well as toes. I enjoy the feel of my toes and the wonder of the complex anatomy of my feet and their fluid, mobile structure. I sway gently, from side to side and to and fro to arrive at a mid-point, an easy, quiet standing position.

One of my favourite phrases for God is Ground of Being. I love the solidity of that as a phrase, the immovable and earthy there-ness of it. One of the things I teach most as an Alexander teacher is the ability to trust the ground beneath us, to give ourselves to the ground. Mostly, strange though this may seem, we don't *do* that. In little ways, we hold ourselves up. We hunch our shoulders, grip our arms against our ribs, curl our toes away from the ground, pull in or push forward or lock our knees back. What we seem to find hard is to simply stand quietly, trusting the ground to hold us up and enjoying the pleasure of just standing, looking up and out, and breathing without interfering with the rise and fall of our body with each breath. As we age, we often see gravity as an enemy, bending us over, pulling us down. But gravity is our friend, rooting us to the earth and letting us find support, to lean on, to stand firm.

Usually, when I teach, the spiritual side of the Alexander work is implicit rather than explicit. I will speak of it if asked but unless it arises naturally, I don't particularly refer to it. However, if I am working with a person of faith—or running a workshop on prayer and Alexander—then I may explicitly raise this point of the value of learning to trust the ground as a spiritual discipline. If I can't trust the ground, which I can not only see but feel, how can I possibly trust the Divine, which cannot be seen? As Richard Rohr says, 'the spiritual experience is about trusting that when you stop holding yourself, Inherent Goodness will still uphold you. Many of us call that God, but you don't have to. It is the trusting that is important'.[26]

And the joy of having the Alexander work as a tool, a companion on the spiritual journey is that I can practise trust in a very concrete way, moment by moment. I can notice if I am pulling myself up or trying too hard and I can let go, which is simultaneously a physical, emotional, mental and spiritual act of trusting the ground, trusting my environment, trusting the air I am given to breathe, and trusting the Divine Ground of Being, because 'the language of spiritual transformation is already written deeply within our bodies.[27] Alexander work is one way of rediscovering that language.

## Trusting My Own Being

Alexander work also helps me to trust my physical structures, which are 'fearfully and wonderfully made' (Psalm 139:14), and to appreciate and care for them. My physical self—skeleton, muscles, organs, blood, nervous system—aren't 'things' to be trained, disciplined or ignored. 'They' are me, made in the image of the Divine, miraculous and extraordinary. And I can listen to what they tell me. Alexander work, like other somatic disciplines is based on the idea that we can learn to be more sensitive to our felt, sensed, and experienced physical selves.

And so, as I learn more about my felt, experienced physical self (and it is a lifelong study because we and the world around us are all constantly changing) I begin to appreciate more and more how extraordinary each human being is. And that helps me to trust a bit more; to trust myself and the wisdom of my physical self, to trust my students' ability to learn and change and grow, and to trust God, in whose image these miraculous physical creatures are made.

## The Challenge of Rest

My observation is that, in today's rather driven society, there are complex and often unexamined emotions attached to the word 'rest'. One of these is guilt. A K Schaffner in her book *Exhaustion, A History*,[28] discusses what is referred to as the Protestant work ethic: the sense that comfort, indulgence, sensual pleasure and, above all, rest are somehow sinful. Today, we have for the most part let go of the idea of the sinfulness of comfort and sensual pleasures, but we seem to have retained, even intensified, a sense that rest is wrong and something to feel guilty about. If I do not try as hard as I can, and fill each moment with productive activity, then I am lazy, sinful, and somehow a bad human being.

And for many people, that attitude of needing always to be productive applies not only to their working lives but to the rest of their lives too. So, high achievement or 'self-improvement' becomes the aim of hobbies and sports. And even our children, if we have them, need to be high achieving so that they reflect well on us. In everything we aim at an illusory *perfection* and mistrust an activity that we do simply for pleasure or just because it's the right thing to do.

We also aim at maximisation. It seems self-evident in modern society that we should earn as much as possible, be as successful as possible, grow our businesses or our churches as large as possible and this is an unquestionable 'good'.

Along with a sense of guilt and the need for maximising our use of time, there may also be anxiety. If I don't fill each moment with activity perhaps I will fail to live up to others' expectations of me, fail my expectations of myself, and fail economically, or professionally. Or, I may simply be afraid of stillness, of silence, of being quiet. Rest, then, becomes rather a challenge for some of us. Perhaps it is something that even requires courage in a world and a society that sees it as either sinful or a sign of weakness.

Yet, physically, rest is a necessity. All organisms need it to recuperate and flourish. As Schaffner points out, fatigue can be understood as a warning sign that our body is being overtaxed and needs to rest.[29] Ignoring those signals consistently may lead to illness or injury in humans or animals. Ignoring the need of the land or the sea to rest is leading to the destruction of our climate and ecosystems.

And because we are physical, emotional, and spiritual beings, rest is a spiritual necessity too. Christianity and Judaism have at their heart a God who rests, a God who worked hard for six days, then took a day off to rest. Not, according to Sam Wells, vicar of St Martin-in-the-Fields, because God was tired, but to allow for contemplation and the enjoyment of creation.[30]

Note that the opposite of restful is restless. The Divine is restful, not restless and desires that restfulness for creation itself. The Divine is not a workaholic. The Divine is not anxious about the need to produce more and more. The well-being of God's creation does not depend on endless work.[31] God commanded humans to rest and extended that command to include animals and even the land itself. The need for rest was enshrined, for the whole of creation, in the concept of the Sabbath. More, harder, longer, faster is not always the right thing to do.

Our restless culture makes it harder for us, as individuals, to rest. So we might need courage to dare to be counter-cultural and rest when we need to. We might also need a particularly Franciscan virtue, *humility*.

## Resting from Doing It All

Humility is not a popular concept. When I was working in schools on character strengths and virtues,[32] I discovered that children and young people associate the word 'humility' with humiliation. Like rest itself, it is seen as a sign of weakness; however, St Francis didn't mind being seen as weak. He was uninterested in success. The word Friar means 'little brother'. Francis was content to be the 'little' brother, both of all people and of creation itself. He never sought power for himself or his brothers, either through economic or political means. He never thought he was better than anyone or anything else. His brothers were to be poor, to be vulnerable, to be available to everyone, to show love to everyone and everything. In contrast to our growth-obsessed, success-obsessed, maximising society, Francis didn't want his order to grow too large. He wanted people to see friars rarely, to wonder 'at the smallness of their number'.[33] Francis' humility, openness to all and his love are characteristics he shared with Christ himself and they brought Francis joy.

During a recent period of serious illness, I had to learn a bit more about humility and acknowledge a profound need for rest. I simply lacked the strength to do all that I used to do. I also began to notice how my first *thought* on waking was of the list of things to be done that day and how my first *act* on waking was a bracing of my shoulders against the burden of that list. I realised that I was constantly pushing myself, striving to do as much as possible in each day, literally thrusting forward into the day and its challenges and cramming into each moment as much 'productivity' as I could. With a lot less energy available to me, I first of all had to employ the Alexander technique and learn to unbrace my shoulders, because the bracing was, itself, a tiring and unnecessary act.

I also had to reappraise how much I attempted to do every day. Rather than thrust forward or lean in, as the book by Sheryl Sandberg advises,[34] I consciously and very physically practised *not* leaning in. Alexander teachers call this 'staying in your back'. By this we mean keeping a balanced awareness of the whole of ourselves and not forgetting and losing awareness of our feet, our backs and our environment. Because we can't see our backs and are so focused on 'getting the stuff in front of us done' most of us *do* forget our backs, and indeed the rest of our physical selves, most of the time. We cut off from feeling and sensation and get lost in our thoughts, our tasks and our worries.

Forgetting our feet and our backs, becoming unaware of our surroundings and our bodies, has a physical effect. It can lead to chronic aches and pains and even injury. And it has an emotional effect too. We feel, like Martha in John's Gospel, harried and worried by many things. We can end up living in the future, anxious and stressed, instead of in the 'now' where none of the things we are fretting about are actually happening.

And forgetting our feet and our backs has a spiritual effect too. When I lose that sense of my own frail, sometimes tired body I can become convinced that I am the only person who can fix the world, reform humanity and save the planet. I can torment myself with a sense that I am indispensable, that everything I do is both urgent and essential and that nobody else can possibly do things as well as me. This is, of course, almost certainly not true and it can lead to burnout. In spiritual terms, it is a form of pride and bad for the ego, as well as for my calendar and my health. It is a tendency I am particularly prone to and one for which I need all the help I can get, from the Alexander technique and the example of St Francis and St Clare.

Humility reminds me that what I do just maybe isn't that important. Nor is it particularly important that I succeed or achieve perfection or be the centre of attention. Perhaps, just perhaps, I could remember the quiet, stable goodness of St Clare, and stop rushing around, always finding places to go and people to see! Perhaps I might remember that, in Christian terms, the Holy Spirit can, in fact, manage without *me*! My work is just to do what is given to me to do now, in this place, as well as I can. So, I try to remember to ask the question, daily and many times a day, what should I do *now*? What is necessary? Or even IS this necessary? And to ask it in an open, enquiring spirit, trusting that what Richard Rohr refers to as 'the Source' will communicate with me, wants to communicate with me, knows me more intimately than I know myself, feet, back and all. He says that 'people who are connected to the Source do not need to steer their own life and agenda. They know that it is being done for them in a much better way than they ever could. Those who hand themselves over are received and the flow happens through them'.[35]

The Alexander technique is about habit—about noticing habits and changing them if we choose to. Having noticed my habits of rather driven over-productivity, of multi-tasking, I am working to stop, to press the pause button on multi-tasking and to foster a new habit, what Dewey calls an intelligently controlled,[36] or conscious habit of doing just one thing at a time and taking pleasure in it.

I am exploring the art of allowing each activity to be surrounded, when possible, by a period of rest and reflection. In Alexander work you learn to be aware of when you are using more muscular effort than you need to use and when you fail to return to a quiet, resting state after each muscular exertion. When I was ill, I had to learn to walk more quietly, work more quietly, and talk to other people without bracing my shoulders and tensing my neck. Because otherwise I soon used up the limited strength my illness had left me. I had to let my whole self, not just my muscles, enjoy returning to quiet after an activity.

That helped me to see the various things that I do more clearly and to value them more. Because I cut back from running four Alexander groups in a week to running one, I realised just how much I love my Alexander group members. Rather than experiencing the burden of running four groups, I discovered the joy of running one. Because I stopped going for a run every day and went for gentle strolls instead, perhaps running *very* slowly once a week, I came to enjoy the pleasure of those strolls, that single slow jog, very acutely.

I often fail. I fail to do one thing at a time, caught up once more in the powerful habit of multi-tasking, and I sometimes fail to rest when I need to or to lean restfully either on the Divine or on the ground, for that matter. And I fail to hand myself over and do less or go quietly and easily through the day. However, I set these intentions very deliberately and try to remember that it is actually the Spirit's job to build the kin-dom of heaven. It is my job and my joy just to join in.

## Resting from Doing It Alone

Not only can it require humility to admit that we need to rest and cannot do everything, but it can also require humility to admit that we cannot do everything *alone*. We need help. My recent illness was also a time when I had to learn, not just to do less, but to ask for help with what I still attempted to do. Not only did I cut back on the number of Alexander groups I was running from four to one, but because I had no real choice, I let my single remaining Alexander group know that I was fairly ill, low in energy and that they would therefore need to help me.

And during the ten-week term, when I was at my weakest, I experienced what I can only describe as grace—unearned, unachieved, undeserved help. A spiritual gift. The group sessions seemed to run themselves. They were frequently immense fun and always left me feeling better than I had at the start. Alexander teachers will speak of 'getting out of the way' and 'letting the right thing do itself'. I had no option but to get out of the way of my group and allow each session to run itself. And it did. And our study of this work and the maturity of the group as a learning community blossomed precisely because I had to learn to lean on them, to do less, to trust them and to rest.

My group became not just my helpers but my teachers in a way I have not experienced in thirty years of working in education. At one of my lowest points, I learned to rest on the kindness, wisdom and goodness of other humans, to study *with* them and be *with* them, rather than doing something *to* them.

There is a humility implicit in the Alexander technique, which is perhaps paradoxical as my impression of its founder, F M Alexander, is that he was not a particularly humble man. This humility is present in the fact that it is difficult, if not impossible, to learn the Alexander technique on your own. Books can be profoundly helpful, but fundamentally humans need other humans in order to be well, and this is especially true of Alexander work. We cannot see ourselves from behind or in profile and it is hard to sense our own areas of tension and to release them. The skilled touch of an Alexander teacher is essential if we are serious about using Alexander work on our path through life.

One of the many, puzzling but rewarding aspects of Alexander work, for me, is my ongoing need for such help. Though I trained full-time for three years, gaining some 1,600 hours of experience, I still find that a skilled colleague can track down and help me to release tension and find more ease, more quietness than I can achieve alone.

Sometimes that frustrates me. However, fundamentally it is another, very physical metaphor for the fact that humans need other humans. I now realise that it is a gift. Neither in my Alexander work, nor in my spiritual life, can I go it alone. Individualism will not help me here. I need colleagues, I need teachers. I need help. And acceptance of the need for help is in itself, an example of the counter-cultural nature of both Alexander and the path of St Francis and St Clare.

# Embodied Prayer Practice: Rest

Julian of Norwich said that the best prayer is to rest in the goodness of God knowing that goodness can reach right down to our lowest depth of need.[37] So try this rest as a prayer.

Sit in a reasonably firm and upright chair if you have one. Put your hands under you and feel your 'sitting bones', the bony bits on the bottom of the pelvis. Now lay your hands gently on your thighs. Imagine your weight flowing through your sitting bones into the chair. Let your feet rest on the floor. Let your back rest against the chair. Your back is touching the chair and the chair is touching your back. Notice all these areas that are touching you, supporting you and take a moment to rest, to feel supported, to be grateful to gravity and to the chair and to the ground that are supporting you.

If it helps you, imagine that you are resting not only on the chair and the ground but in the arms of the Divine, of Love, or the Universe. Held, supported, and cared for.

Or, if you are very tired, or sitting is uncomfortable, lie down on a firm but comfortable surface and let the ground support you notice the ground touching your body and your body touching the ground...

Rest a while....

# Embodied Prayer Practice: Stand Firm

Richard Rohr notes that St Clare lived for forty years in one place, outside the town of Assisi, called San Damiano. He calls her a master and mistress of letting go of all that was unnecessary or unimportant.[38]

Clare, quite literally, stood in one place for the whole of her life, leaning on the strength of God. She turned down the efforts of popes, patrons or sponsors to endow her and her sisters with money or property, and thereby confer status upon them *and* control them. She stood firm and remained simple and free.

Practice the simple prayer of standing firm. You can find a wall to stand against if that helps. Indeed, standing against a wall can be a good thing to do regularly since it helps you to find an easy, upright standing position.

Have the intention of standing quietly, easily. Be aware of where your balance is and try to let it be evenly spread into both feet and the ground beneath. Have your feet comfortably as far apart as your hips, or slightly less. Let your legs be straight. Let the ground support you. Be aware of both your weight falling into the ground and of the support from the ground flowing up your back and up the front of you and out through the top of your head. Let your gaze soften and widen. Let go of the need to go anywhere, to do anything and just stand... in the light of Love, on the Ground of Being, held, cared for, and safe.

## Chapter 4

# Help Me to Meet Others

### Joyously

In the Third Order, we work to make space for three qualities in our lives—love, joy and humility. I say we work to make space for them because we regard them as 'graces', or gifts, not things we can acquire or achieve through our own efforts. We have practices, like prayer and living simply, that are intended to open us to those gifts, but we don't make them happen ourselves. We *receive* them, we *allow* them to take root and grow in us, we notice that they are there and we feel thankful for them. We even *surrender* to them. But we can't make them happen.

I find a parallel here with the Alexander principle of direction, which is making physical changes indirectly through allowing, rather than through direct muscular effort. Throughout our training, Alexander teachers are told, 'no don't *do* it, *think* it' and allow it to happen. To begin with, this is both puzzling and frustrating—at least, I found it so; however, gradually we do learn to *think* rather than to do, and this is the basis of the Alexander technique.

Alexander realised that if he tried, directly, to make changes to his movements he produced more, not less, of the tension that was giving him speech problems. So he developed a series of verbalised commands or thoughts that focused his attention and promoted more coordinated movement; '*allow* the neck to be free to *let* the head go forward and up so that the back *may* lengthen and widen'.[39] These directions, as they are termed, are still taught to students today, and they are all indirect statements about *allowing* and *letting* change happen, not about directly trying to do something differently.

Just as the Third Order acknowledge that love, joy and humility are gifts, not things we can produce directly, and just as the Alexander technique is based on the principle of allowing the right thing to happen, rather than trying to *make* it happen, so John Dewey (an early 20ᵗʰ-century thinker on democracy and education) argued that teachers never teach anything directly; instead they teach indirectly, through the environment they create.[40] This means that Alexander teachers, and indeed all teachers, require a large dose of the humility that characterised Francis. In one sense we are not teaching anything at all. We are simply creating an environment where the 'other' can flourish and can learn about themselves. Our work as teachers is fundamentally indirect.

Of course, in other senses, we are teaching constantly. We are using our voice, our body, our understanding, our touch, and our thinking to create as much clarity and opportunity for insight as we can. But all teaching is directed at influencing the environment so that, within it, students can learn. It is indirectly creating a space where change can occur. Everything that a teacher says, does and thinks, every nuance of their voice and movement is creating an effect, influencing the environment, moment by moment. It is a huge responsibility and privilege to accept the role and the vocation of 'teacher', of any subject, in any human society. But it is also a joyful role, and joy is an important part of education, as well as of the Christian life.

## Joy in Teaching

I have been given the gift of an extraordinary Alexander group in the past few years. I have been teaching them regularly in Manchester for nearly ten years and though the membership changes slightly term by term there is a core of regular members. The generous, open, curious study of Alexander by these members, along with the developing friendships, keeps the group warm and welcoming to newcomers yet secure and rooted in the practices of learning we have developed together. And as I have learned to trust the group and to trust those practices, to get out of the way and let Reality quietly show itself, we all increasingly seem to experience joy.

Simone Weil, a 20th-century Christian mystic who was also a school teacher, said that intelligence can only be led by desire and only grows and bears fruit in pleasure and joy. She thought that joy in learning was as important as the breath in running.[41] I have come to see joy as a litmus test that indicates that learning—deep learning—is actually happening. Joy does not preclude discomfort, or even confusion and struggle. Joy is vital and strong and robust. And it is a product of community and relationship, not of individualism.

One of the important elements of education for Dewey was that true education has to go two ways: a conversation, not a one-way lecture. He said that all communication and social life is 'educative', and involves sharing experience until it belongs to all those involved and changes each one of them.[42]

When I teach Alexander work, I engage in conversation at different levels. Literally, we are verbally talking at least some of the time, but we also constantly converse non-verbally. Each of us will be picking up unconscious signals from the other person which we respond to, also unconsciously. And we communicate through touch and that communication, again, goes two ways. I am touched by my students and they are touched by me. That is a privilege and a sacred experience.

When I am at my best and I look back on a lesson, perhaps especially a group lesson that went well, I see people appear to grow in confidence. They seem more alive, more open, and often more cheerful and lively at the end of a session than they were at the beginning. When I notice this, I conclude that, with all my imperfections, I have successfully created an environment in which we were all able to learn, to grow and to find a little more space, freedom and enjoyment of life. I see my work as creating a listening, curious, safe and attentive space, and helping people to slow down enough and feel safe enough to notice, to pay attention to what is really there, both in the environment and themselves. This lets them encounter what is really there, which we might also term the Real, God, Providence, or the Spirit. 'Salvation', Rohr says, 'is becoming who you already are'.[43]

My understanding is that it is this encounter with what is really there and with who they really are, that creates the freedom, the aliveness that I notice in my students. And it is that aliveness and freedom which creates joy for all of us.

An essential element in that space is my own conscious willingness for the communication to be two ways so that it can be, as Dewey said, truly 'educative'. For that to happen I must be willing to be changed by my students and my teaching. I must allow my group participants to help and teach me and to help and teach one another. To bring *me* joy. And, once again, that requires humility. Because then, neither the creation of the teaching environment nor the education process is all about me. As far as possible I must try to let go of my own ego, preoccupations and assumptions, and take a step back so that my students can step forward into the space I have just vacated. The model I like best is to aim to be the *little sister* of my Alexander group as Francis was the little brother of creation, all the while being generous with and not undervaluing my experience and prior study.

## Joy in Seeing

The Alexander technique highlights the need to see clearly, to be aware, and that can be a source of joy. However, one of my struggles with the Alexander work, and with its founder and the early teachers of the work, was with what felt like a censorious and judgemental attitude on their part, both towards themselves and towards others. Alexander called his fallible perception

'faulty' or even 'perverted sensory appreciation'.[44] The teachers
I trained with were much more positive in their approach, and
of course, language has changed in many ways since the early
20th century. However, I still worried that, fundamentally, the
Alexander work was judgemental and about seeing and fixing
what was wrong with our students. Alexander himself spoke
of the 'bad manner of use' and the 'physical degeneration' he
saw in most people.[45] As a school teacher with thirty years'
experience before I encountered the Alexander technique, I
baulked at the negativity of the language I heard. I did not want
my focus to be on seeing what was wrong and 'fixing it', either
in myself or others.

I find a tension here between seeing how people, myself
included, can and do distort their own bodies unnecessarily
whilst simultaneously affirming that all that they are is good
and beautiful. Further, if people are in pain because of how they
walk, sit or stand, then I have both a desire and a duty to help
them see reality more accurately, so that they may walk, sit or
stand more gently and easily.

This tension perhaps mirrors tensions in the spiritual
life between judgement and unconditional love, between
contemplation and action, between grace and effort. However, as
I walk my curious Christian/Franciscan/contemplative/Alexander
teaching path I find that I want beauty, love, kindness and
gentleness to be my entry point, more and more. Really, I want to
rejoice when I look at another human being, in the wonder and
miracle that is each person. As Bruce Fertman says to his trainees,
'I want you to see a person's beauty, and through that beauty I
want you next to see and sense their humanity'.[46] My personal
path to learning to see the beauty in each person includes turning
to St Francis and St Clare for help.

What I find in Francis and Clare, that illuminates my
Alexander teaching and constantly reminds me to pause before
attempting to 'fix' somebody, is a profound reverence for all

creatures, human and animal, with faulty sensory perception or otherwise. This feels like a welcome counter balance to the harshness I heard in Alexander's writings and can find in myself. Above all, I find in the Franciscan path a compassionate love that may have been there in Alexander himself, but which was not always apparent to me. St Francis was and is a constant reminder to see the beauty in each person, to see God or the Divine in each person, and so to approach each person with reverence.

The paradox for the teacher is that it is not until we affirm, accept and fully celebrate what our pupil is and where they are *now* that they feel safe enough to let go of that and to move on. Only when I don't wish to 'fix' them can we both learn to be a little freer, a little bit easier, and to walk lightly into the next moment. And that can lead us to joy.

## Being with Others Peacefully

One of my own areas of challenge as a Franciscan Christian is that I am not naturally either open to all or particularly loving. While Bruce Fertman can write that for him, liking people is natural,[47] for me, liking people is *not* natural at all. Rather, my own default response towards other adult humans is one of *fear*, not love. I say other adult humans because, conversely, I am not afraid of small humans, of children. When I am with children, I can be the open, curious, loving, joyful person I would prefer to be. I have the reputation of being 'good with children'. I simply find them interesting; I *like* them. Adults, on the whole, scare me, so my physical, emotional, and spiritual default reaction or habit is to close, to defend myself, to cut myself off.

Cynthia Bourgeault writes of the spiritual path that it is about surrender, inner opening, and handing oneself over. And this is always an act of strength, not weakness. She notes that confronted by any situation in life, whether threat or opportunity, we can respond in one of two ways. We can either brace, harden and resist, or soften, open and yield. 'Spiritual practice at its no-frills simplest is a moment by moment learning not to do anything in a state of internal brace. Bracing is never worth the cost'.[48] My recent illness showed me that not only was I bracing against my long list of usually self-imposed tasks on waking each morning, but I was also bracing whenever I encountered or even thought about encountering any adult humans outside a very small circle. I recognised this slight fear of other people as a long-established, perhaps even lifelong, habit.

Sometimes my fear is obvious to me, I can feel it and recognise it for what it is. At other times it manifests as other emotions, as a lack of confidence, perhaps, or as a doubting both of my abilities and indeed of the value of what I have to offer the world. Above all, it manifests in how tired I get when I am with others for too long. I am tired because my muscles, my tendons, and my whole physical, emotional and spiritual self is working more than is necessary. It is not peaceful, easy, nor joyful.

Sometimes my fear hides itself beneath anger, particularly if others disagree with or challenge me. Because I am afraid of conflict, I almost always suppress this anger and don't allow it to show outwardly, but it will inevitably be present in a certain tension and a lack of peace, a lack of ease, empathy or being able to listen deeply to the other person.

Christians tend to see conflict as evil and an indication of the presence of sin, and certainly part of the Franciscan commitment is to work for peace; however, perhaps paradoxically, peace does not necessarily mean an absence of conflict. Alastair McKay argues that conflict is not only part of God's plan for creation but part of the kingdom of heaven too.[49] His thinking is that conflict arises from diversity plus tension—and diversity is very clearly part of God's creation.

When I first read this, I was shocked by his argument and immediately thought that if we removed tension we would have no conflict. However, I know from my Alexander work that an absence of tension is no better than too much tension. We need tension to move and even to breathe. So, without enough tension, quite literally, we would die. And, as I thought about McKay's surprising argument, I realised that we need conflict too. It is the oppositional forces within the body, along with the essential tensions, that create space, freedom and movement.

One of my current 'learning edges' in my own study of Alexander, and how I apply it in my Christian life, is to let go of my fear and avoidance of conflict and to see it as an opportunity for movement and freedom. And at the same time to hold on to my opinions lightly, to be open to challenge and to be willing to let go of them peacefully, if that seems right. St Francis is said to have told his brothers that if they didn't give up their opinions then they hadn't embraced poverty properly.[50] Humility has to admit that I, even I, might sometimes be wrong!

## Learning from Others Peacefully

The other sense in which I can learn from Francis, Clare and Alexander about how to be with others peacefully, is in my willingness to be open to difference. The human reaction to difference, like my own reaction to other adults, is often fear. We can fear those of different faiths, races, colours, political opinions, sexualities, and genders. I am not immune to that fear. I certainly find challenges to my opinions, beliefs and ideas about what is 'normal' to be, well, challenging! In the area of religion, I am committed to a life path that follows Jesus Christ after the example of Francis and Clare. It is in the light of the truths I find in the Christian story that I interpret my own life and the life of the world. However, that does not mean I cannot find and learn from other truths, expressed in other faiths, other stories. Some Christians believe that Christianity has a monopoly on Truth, but that is not a view I share. Nor, as I understand him at least, did Francis.

There is a beautiful story that is told about St Francis' encounter with Sultan Malik Al-Kamal in 1219. Francis' intention had been to convert the Sultan to Christianity and to end the Fifth Crusade. He went very deliberately through the enemy lines and was captured, beaten and eventually taken into the presence of the Sultan. As he entered the tent, Francis purportedly said, 'Peace be upon you'. In the days that followed the two men spoke and, importantly, *listened* to one another. And then Francis left. The war continued. The Sultan continued to be a Muslim. Francis' mission was, on the surface, a complete failure; however, Francis seemed to have been changed by the encounter, and the two men appeared to have become friends.

Though he refused almost all the gifts the Sultan pressed upon him, Francis accepted one: a horn used by Muslims to call the faithful to prayer. When he returned home Francis used the horn to call his own brothers and sisters to prayer, five times a day, just as the Muslims prayed, five times a day. He also wrote a canticle we call 'The Praises of God'. I heard a talk by one of our First Order Brothers, Nicholas Allen, where he argued that this canticle shows 33 names of God and is evidence for how much Francis was influenced by what he learned from the Sultan about the 99 Names of God.

It is from my own Sufi friends that I have learned more about the very physical nature of prayer and the wisdom and grace of regularly bowing one's forehead to the ground in the face of the Absolute. Karen Armstrong calls Salat, (the Muslim ritual prayer) a 'kenotic, ego-deflating act'.[51] Such physical prayer profoundly embodies an attitude of letting go or self-emptying, which is what kenosis means.

It is also from the Sufi tradition that I have learned of the spiritual power of chant to quieten and clear the mind and to take prayer deep into the body, integrating mind, body and heart. These wisdom practices are present in the Christian tradition,[52] but they are no longer widely taught, and I certainly didn't encounter them during thirty years of active church membership. So, I take from Francis encouragement and permission to learn peacefully and joyfully from those who believe differently and who follow a different path from my own. Francis was changed by his encounter with the Sultan and the basis of the Christian term 'conversion' is to change, to turn around and look in a different direction. I have been changed by becoming friends with Sufi Muslims.

This peaceful openness to change, so evident in Francis, can also be a fruit of the Alexander technique. Dewey, who was a keen student and lifelong friend of F M Alexander, highlighted the intellectual openness that can result from the study of Alexander work. He attributed his own willingness to change his mind in response to new evidence to his studies with Alexander and contrasted this with the defensiveness that too often characterises academics.[53]

Clinging to ideas, particularly religious ideas, risks turning them into idols. I can love and be committed to my faith and still peacefully accept that our images of God are partial, our understandings inadequate, and our interpretations different to those of other people and even from our own former interpretations. In other words, I can be curious and open to new thoughts, new ideas, and new ways of being Christian, whilst secure in my tradition and belief that I am loved. Our beliefs can and, indeed, should change as we age. They should develop and mature. We can peacefully meet new ideas as they arise, thinking about and testing them in our spiritual lives and communities.

In my Third Order office, we pray, 'Give us a true faith, a certain hope and a perfect love'.[54] I like that prayer. And what I like most about it is that certainty is applied not to faith, but to hope. Richard Rohr says that the opposite of faith is not doubt, but certainty or the need for it.[55] He says scriptures don't offer us certainty but, instead, a different way of knowing, a pathway and an intimate relationship where we can discover for ourselves the necessity of grace, love, mercy and forgiveness in an uncertain world.[56]

I have a certain *hope*, though, not a certain *faith*. I am, quite definitely, a hopeful person and I see Christianity as a profoundly hope-filled faith. And that hope is a certain one, a solid one, a true one that has been tested and found reliable by many, many people wiser and better than I, for many, many years.

I peacefully live with an uncertain faith that admits doubt, mystery and wonder. I see Christianity as true yet mysterious, reliable yet challenging, dependable yet exciting and both life-giving and worth living for. I make my spiritual home in Christianity and it is a home with a sure foundation. I also pray that I will remain *true*, which is to say faithful and loyal, to the Christian and Franciscan path that I will love to the end of my days. And there is peace in that.

# Embodied Prayer Practice: Opening

St Augustine says that sin is being curved in upon oneself.[57] When we physically curve in on ourselves, we curl up, like a fern. The opposite of curving in, is opening up, or unfurling.

Try that in your own body. First curl up, like a fern. Then unfurl and keep gently unfurling until you are looking up and out to the world and your arms are spread wide to all that is. Don't stretch; be gentle with your body and stay comfortable and soft and open. And smile. That is a prayer.

# Embodied Prayer Practice: Reading a Poem Aloud

As I will explore in another Embodied Prayer Practice, the act of reading aloud is quite different from silent reading. It is an act, a physical speech act that changes the world around us and changes us. Try to cultivate the practice of reading poetry aloud and allow it to change you.

I love this poem by the priest Richard Carter. It summarises much of what I am trying to say in this book. Read it aloud as prayer:

## Joy

The less longing
The more presence
The less we bang on the door, the more it opens for us
The less we demand, the more we can open our eyes to the
    beauty of gift
The less we expect, the greater the joy and surprise
The more selfless, the more self
Clamorous need shuts us off from the needed
It is our clinging which is our death
The less we cling, the more we embrace
The less we fear, the more we love
All joy reminds us
It is never a possession, it is always behind us and before us
And our love a taste of things to come
Go lightly
Go simply
A breathing out
A breathing in

A shared breath
A letting go
That we may be held forever.

Richard Anthony Carter

# Chapter 5

# Help Me to Wait

## Waiting Patiently

At the heart of the Alexander technique are two key principles known as 'inhibition' and 'direction'. Inhibition is the ability *not* to react automatically to a stimulus. It is a profound muscular and neurological 'stopping' or quietening of our whole self that lets us observe and change deep-seated, unhelpful habits. Direction is influencing our physical selves through conscious thought, awareness or imagery, rather than through direct muscular effort.

Over the past years, I have increasingly come to see these core principles of the Alexander work as a contemplative practice that can be used in my own faith tradition, Christianity, as well as in others. They help me to quieten down and to practise waiting on God, waiting for God, and they physically embody that waiting on, and for, God in my life.

## Learning Patiently

When I was working regularly in schools on a well-being project called Celebrating Strengths,[58] we used a list of character strengths and virtues inspired by the field of positive psychology that arose in the USA in 1999.[59] The original list of 24 strengths or virtues contained words like love, kindness, persistence, humility, and spirituality. Patience, however, was nowhere to be seen, as the UK teachers I worked with invariably pointed out. And because patience is an essential virtue in both teaching and learning I added it to the list that I worked with in my particular project.

Patience is essential to teaching and education not just because of the need to be patient with students and, indeed, with ourselves as fallible teachers. It is essential because at the core of learning is a willingness to wait, patiently and to live with unknowing for long enough for knowing to emerge. Learning takes time. John Keats called this kind of patience *negative capability*, a willingness to live with doubt and uncertainty.[60]

For me, patience is also essential to the practice of the spiritual life. Union with God is not something I can or even need to achieve or do or make happen because it already exists. I am in God, and so is the whole of creation, and God is in me. The work of contemplation is gradually to open my eyes to who I already am, and what Reality already is and always has been. My practice creates the conditions in which growth can happen, in which my eyes can gradually open more and more; but I don't make growth happen, it just does. My task is to continue with the practices that help me let go of needing to be the centre of my own life, of needing to get my own way. My task is to keep turning up.

Spiritual traditions sometimes speak of this need for getting my own way as the false self, small self or ego.[61] It is the self that splits the world happily into good (me) and bad (anyone who disagrees with me), and into male/female, self/other, nature/nurture, black/white, right/wrong and good/evil dichotomies. The spiritual path is seen as a way of integrating and transcending the self so that we can be in touch with an essential self, a *true* self.[62]

I like the word 'integrating'. The Alexander technique is sometimes described as a work which helps us to find more integration, to experience mind and body working in unity, to move, think and feel as a whole, not as a collection of parts, whether that is legs and arms and head or mind and body. In the Alexander work this essential unity is sometimes called 'primary control'.

Maggie Ross uses the word 'trans-figure', rather than transcend. She says that the work of silence is about learning to see differently, literally to change how we figure things out, how we behold ourselves, others and the world.[63] Silence, contemplation, the Alexander work, changes what we pay attention to and how we pay attention. Sin, which I think is, perhaps, what the Alexander world means by 'poor use', is not actually *being* separate from the Divine, for everything is held within the Divine Reality. There is nowhere else to be. Rather, sin is the *illusion* of separation, of *seeing* ourselves as separate. Sin is experiencing ourselves, falsely, as separate. It is being unconscious of the fact that we share the Divine nature, that we are Holy or Whole or One.

My work, (and many spiritual paths, including the Alexander technique, do tend to be referred to as 'the Work') is then to learn to see differently and, above all, to wait for the Divine nature to act in and through me. My spiritual practice, which includes the Alexander technique, is intended to help me learn to see differently. In Christian terms, this is what is meant by conversion or living 'in Christ'. It is what Franciscans mean by poverty. A profound letting go of the self and my illusion of separation. A simple willingness to be still and neither hide nor close my eyes, which Clare lived out so well, so that God can look at, love and work within me, teaching me to gradually see with Her eyes and love who and what She loves.

When Alexander practitioners use the term 'good use' they tend to mean physical integration, easy movement, poise, and, yes, it can mean all of that. But I think it can mean much more.

## Waiting Patiently

I found it hard to understand the Alexander principle of inhibition when I was training, partly because I lacked patience, of course. I wanted to understand and to understand *now*. And partly it is because inhibition IS hard to understand. I now see that it is a profound lifelong study and quality of being, rather than a simple technique to master. It is a quality of quietness and awareness from which movement can occur or which can continue as stillness. As long as we live, we can go deeper and deeper into that quiet, spacious, stillness. However, when I needed to make sense of it during my early lessons, I borrowed an idea from David Steindl-Rast, a Benedictine monk, who said that pausing right before and right after an action has the effect of 'decompressing time' and centring us.[64] This became my early understanding of inhibition and continues, I hope, to be a good introduction to a profound skill. Alexander called it preventing the too-quick and unthinking response. Other Alexander teachers use words like 'pausing, coming back to quiet, composing ourselves, the conscious intention not to do something, not reacting with the old habit'.[65]

Coming to quiet is a favourite phrase of mine when I am teaching, but I also encourage my students to be aware of the ground beneath them and the contact of their feet with the floor. I suggest they notice if they are trusting the ground or holding themselves up. When they notice and *stop* holding themselves up then they are practising inhibition.

What frustrated me in my own training was how hard it was to grasp what inhibition means once we are moving. Yes, I can pause before action. But what does it mean to inhibit while I am *in* action? My current understanding is that what I am inhibiting, or stopping, is actually mindlessness or distraction, a lack of awareness of the present moment. I am inhibiting the mind's tendency to drift out of the present and into the past or to race ahead into the future and, hence, to become oblivious to birdsong, wind and the simple joy and gift of each footstep I take and each breath that enters my body. I inhibit the powerful temptation to disappear into my screen and my virtual reality and leave my physical self and environment behind. I inhibit forgetfulness of all that is.

I have to be patient with myself and practise a moment by moment noticing and remembering when I have forgotten, yet again, returning to the present, again and again and again. And I need to do that patiently, inhibiting judgement, inhibiting yelling at myself or thinking that I need to be other than, or somehow better than I am now. Instead, I need to patiently practise noticing the ground, the birdsong, and the room I occupy. It is a lovely practice because I am learning not to forget or be blind to the joy of each moment. But it *is* a practice! It is work, albeit a gentle, beautiful work.

## Waiting Serenely

According to the dictionary definition, 'serenely' means calmly, peacefully or untroubled. The other side of the Alexandrian coin from inhibition, or stopping and coming to quiet, is the word, 'direction'. Alexander realised that trying to directly change his long-seated physical and mental habits around reciting on stage just made things worse. He learned first to stop, to inhibit, his former habits and then to *think* what it was he wanted to happen. Fundamentally, he learned to stop trying so hard to be right.

He called this kind of thinking, 'direction'. Alexander developed a series of phrases that discouraged undue tension and, instead, encouraged a coordinated, integrated, easy movement. They allowed him to speak and breathe as well as to move with more awareness and fluidity. The phrases he bequeathed to his students are: 'Neck to be free, head to go forward and up, back to lengthen and widen, knees to go forward and away'.[66]

Again, as with inhibition, one's understanding of what direction really means is hard to put into words and changes over time. What it does imply, though, is that we don't focus so much on reaching the goal itself that we lose sight of how we can achieve it. Once our goal is decided on, then, to an extent, we remain unattached to the results of the action and stay conscious of the process—the means that are used to attain the goal. It is paying attention to *how* we do what we do, not just to *what* we do. And we remain calm and, in a sense, trusting, that a coordinated movement or action will flow from us giving our directions, from stopping and thinking.

The way that I relate this to my Franciscan path is that I focus on what I need to do now and try not to focus too much on the future. Nor do I worry unduly about the success, or otherwise, of the projects that I engage with or the work that I do. This doesn't mean that I don't try to do the best that I can, because I do. But I ask myself *how* I am doing what I am doing. Am I working creatively, kindly, collaboratively, and lovingly? And when failure or setback occurs, when things stop, as they stopped in the midst of the Covid-19 pandemic, I try to quietly let them go, trusting that, in the long run, 'all will be well and all will be well and all manner of thing shall be well'.[67] And that is the sense in which I understand waiting serenely.

Where, though, does serenity and waiting leave the Christian struggle for justice? Certainly, Clare and Francis worked hard to alleviate suffering. Clare famously worked even on her sick bed. There is a story of her dropping her sewing and being too weak to retrieve it. A large convent cat fetched it for her, which is why, in her icons, she is often pictured with a rather fine black cat!

So, serenity does not mean that I am not troubled, that I do not care, that I do not work for justice. Francis was often moved to tears by the pain he saw around him, and he worked to relieve suffering, as we all should. And he was also often moved to laughter, to song and to praise. Clare and Francis chose to challenge injustice by living differently and by holding fast to a profound trust that, one day, all would be well and the kin-dom of heaven would come.

And ultimately that is why I think serenity can be a gift of the Christian path and the Franciscan path in particular. We are part of a long story, longer than our own lifetime, longer than our own world, bigger than the latest crisis or political controversy or even natural disaster. Our part is to quietly do the next thing, within that story, that we are given to do, and then the next and the next. And it is not really our job to worry about results, successes or failures. That is my understanding of the Franciscan path, and it seems to me that it is pure Alexander technique too.

Much of the work of learning the Alexander technique, either as student or teacher, boils down to learning to say *no*. No to habit, no to reacting in a too quick and unthinking way to what happens around us. No to doing more than we need in terms of effort and activity. Here again, there is a curious spiritual parallel. The environmentalist Bill McKibben says that human lives are the most curious on the planet because we can destroy, but also because we can decide not to destroy. Animals act on instinct, but humans can exercise restraint. He calls it our superpower, albeit one we exercise all too seldom. We can and we are wrecking the planet, but we can also choose not to.[68]

McKibben refers to this human restraint as love. And I think that inhibition can be love, or at least can make space and time for love. Space for a loving and gentle respect for my own embodied self. Space for a loving awareness of my environment and how to gently interact with it. And space for a loving, quiet respect for all creatures, including my human sisters and brothers and siblings, a respect that sees our interconnectedness, our utter equality in the sight of God and our infinite value. We inhibit, we say no, to seeing others as a means of self-fulfilment. We say no to putting money and things before people. We say no to being always too busy to have time for friends and family or to watch birds or smell flowers. We say no to a politics that treats people as economic units and is based on competition, on winners and losers, on exploiting people and our planet for short-term gain. We say no to all of that — serenely.

During my training, my gentle, kind and humble teacher, Malcolm Williamson, would often quote his teacher, Walter Carrington (1915–2005) and his various sayings. And one of the sayings that I really liked, and continue to use is, 'do only what is necessary and take the time that it takes'. When the Covid-19 pandemic arrived and churches in my country were closed, many of us rushed around like the proverbial headless chicken having meetings, learning how to operate Zoom Sunday services and live-stream morning prayer on the internet. And we tried to do all of that as rapidly as possible. And it can be argued that good things came of that flurry of activity, that rapid response. We could argue that we were meeting local needs.

However, I was particularly impressed by the response of one church which was—to wait and to be still.[69] They did not exactly do nothing, but they did only what they felt was absolutely necessary. The leaders encouraged people to meet, think, still and reflect on what they were learning from this experience. They resisted the natural human urge to respond to disaster with a flurry of activity and instead followed the command of Psalm 46 to 'Be still and know that I am God'. I find I have to ask myself, as I reflect on that time, how much of my own activity was a way of distracting myself from the sadness and the helplessness that humans feel when confronted with genuine suffering and real loss? It is frankly easier to be busy than to be still. When I am busy, I can forget that I am mortal, that my motives are always mixed, that those I love, and all humans are fragile creatures who easily suffer and die and who live brief lives. Being busy helps me to feel important, immortal, and at the centre of things!

I feel now that the response of this church was perhaps wiser, deeper, and more trusting than my own. And perhaps too, in the long run, it might achieve more than others who leapt forward without thinking, without pausing to ask *how* they were doing what they were doing—and if it was necessary? Was it what was called for—*now*?

When we pause, when we stop being busy, we can ask ourselves who we really are when there is no more rushing around?

## Waiting for the Unfolding of Thy Will

A pet hate of many clergy is the request for Frank Sinatra's 'I Did it My Way' at church funerals. This might seem a little harsh, but it is a song that seems to go against the whole thrust of the spiritual life and teachings of Christ, which is to let *thy* will be done, not mine at all! Western individualism is all about me doing *my* thing, me succeeding, meeting my potential, doing what I want to do how and when I want to do it. Yet, the Christian life is about letting go of *me* and *mine* in favour of the Divine will, in favour of Thee and Thou, in favour of *we* and *us*.

Though the Alexander work has what is, for me and some others, a very obvious spiritual dimension to it, not a great deal has been written about this. In part, that is what I am attempting to do here. One book that does look at this area is *F. Matthias Alexander and the Creative Advance of the Individual* by George Bowden, a voice teacher and keen student of the Alexander technique. He draws parallels between the Alexander technique and Zen, noting how in Zen archery the student learns to let an action happen indirectly and spontaneously. He references Herrigel's *Zen in the Art of Archery*[70] which relates how, following what seemed a causal, almost unthinking aim, the Master rose, bowed, smiled and said, 'Just then It shot!'[71]

Bowden equates this to the sensation that a student of Alexander work has when a movement happens almost (but not quite) by itself, something that we sometimes refer to as non-doing. Alexander spoke of 'letting the neck be free' not of freeing the neck. Our focus is indirect, on getting out of the way. Then the question arises, of course, getting out of *whose* way, or *what's* way? If *It* shot in the example of Zen archery, what is *It*, exactly? It is common to hear very secular and physical explanations for this. 'It' is variously referred to as poise, good use, postural tone, or our natural way of doing something. I see none of these as incorrect. For me, however, they are incomplete.

What Bowden does in his book is to take another step with the implications of *It* within a theistic, rather than Buddhist, worldview by saying, quite simply and succinctly that the Alexander technique is a method for consciously putting into actual, concrete practice the prayer 'thy will, not mine be done'.[72]

Bowden also points out that, in the Anglican liturgy we begin morning prayer by saying 'O Lord, open thou our lips'.[73] We don't open our lips ourselves; we ask God to open them for us! And the net result of waiting, of being patient, of letting go of the need to open my own lips and speak my own words, is that 'our mouths shall declare your praise'. When we are still, patient and quiet an energy, a vibrant song and dance of life arises and pours out of us. That is the Alexander technique at its best; that is prayer; that is praise.

Cynthia Bourgeault writes about kenosis, meaning the act of letting go or emptying oneself.[74] The *self* that is to be emptied refers to the small self we think of as separate, that wants its own way in all things, that worries about *self*-image and craves *self*-indulgence. I learned recently that the Hebrew word *salvation* can be translated as a wide, open space of endless freedom. The goal, then, of letting go of that small self is to see with different eyes, to be free of the illusion that I am separate from God. It is to see that I am part of a wider and more connected reality, a wide, open space and to be free enough to enjoy what Bourgeault calls an inner quality of aliveness.[75] That inner aliveness is the gift of the spiritual life and is available to everyone, every moment of every day.

The spiritual life, the serene waiting, then becomes much less a question of thinking the right things or mentally arm wrestling myself into believing every dot and semicolon of Scripture and tradition. Nor is it really about acquiring skills or new accomplishments or engaging in acts or performances that please God. It is rather a moment-by-moment, very physical opening of myself, a handing over of all that I am to what IS, to Reality, to Love, to the Ground of my being. It is a letting go, a surrendering, a stopping and a resting in the presence of the Divine. And I can stop by learning to notice, to pay attention to where I am, to the ground that supports me and to accept what comes in life with trust that I am supported and will always be supported—by the ground, by the Divine, by the breath in my body.

Bourgeault says that when we open or soften, when we don't brace, a Divine being can reach us. 'Going with the softness, the yes, always connects you immediately with your heart, and then the divine intelligence can begin to operate'.[76]

The Alexander technique is one tool I can use moment by moment. It is ideal. There are no set times I have to 'practise' Alexander, other than *all* the time. There are no set exercises I need to make space for in my daily routine and remember to do them. It is about how I do *everything*, all the time. It is the perfect companion for walking the spiritual path of surrender, for learning to soften and open and say *yes*, to others, to the world, to my own amazing gift of being alive, to God.

Before encountering the Alexander work and becoming Franciscan, I very much resisted the teaching of Christ that 'unless a grain of wheat falls into the ground and dies it remains just a single grain, but if it dies it bears much fruit. Those who love their life lose it, and those who hate their life in this world will keep it for eternal life' (John 12:24–25). I used to see these teachings as negative and troubling. Now I see them as being about letting go of the illusion that I am separate and that I am alone, with letting go of the need to fix the world, my life and the lives of those around me. I see them as the pearl of great price, as not only beautiful but profoundly true in my experience, and certainly as the way to living a richer, fuller, kinder and gentler life.

# Embodied Prayer Practice: The Soft Gaze

Physically speaking, there are two main ways of looking. A narrow, convergent gaze that fixes on an object. Or a wide expansive, less fixed gaze that takes in the distance and the periphery. According to Meir Schneider, who teaches what he calls yoga for the eyes, the modern world over encourages the former at the expense of the latter.[77] The net result of too much use of the fixed, narrow gaze is a lot of tension. It also means that we often fail to notice the birds, the sunshine, the blue of the sky, a passer-by's smile of greeting.

So, try going for a walk with a soft, wide gaze. Allow the world to come to your eyes, make your gaze consciously gentler and appreciative—notice the beauty around you. Let it come to you and give thanks for it.

# Embodied Prayer Practice: Kneeling to Pray

Karen Armstrong says that Islam is, above all, a way of life, a call to practical compassion, something people *do*. And one of the things that Muslims are called to do is to prostrate their bodies to the ground five times a day, a practice called Salat.

Christians, too, used to kneel regularly for prayer, recognising, rightly, that the habitual postures we assume to pray do affect, drop by drop, our inner attitudes and the quality of our prayer. It is harder, though of course still possible, to remain proud and full of oneself while kneeling and bowing one's forehead to the ground regularly.

In the Orthodox Christian tradition, believers will lie full length on the floor with arms outstretched in the shape of a cross. Cynthia Bourgeault tells a lovely story of a young man who went to the Russian Orthodox archbishop, Anthony Bloom, full of despair because the creeds of Christianity made him angry and its dogma and theology seemed stupid, yet he longed for a life of faith. The archbishop told him to go home and practise one hundred full prostrations every day for a month. Intrigued, if puzzled, the young man did so and when he returned, he was no longer angry but full of a joyful faith. The faith that had eluded his mind had taken root in his body.[78]

If you can, introduce or reintroduce a practice of kneeling into your spiritual discipline, Christian or otherwise. Remember to be gentle with your body and listen to it. If you kneel, do so easily, lovely. Perhaps find a kneeling stool or bench to take the weight off your feet. They are readily available online. Do whatever you need to make yourself comfortable. Discomfort is *not* a good idea, neither in prayer nor at any other time. Always practise kindness towards your embodied self. It is a gift and we need to take care of it.

If you cannot kneel, don't worry. Sports science shows us that vividly imagining ourselves doing something can be as effective as actually doing it, just as the Alexander technique teaches us that thinking profoundly influences our body. In this case, sit quietly and gently upright one or more times a day and close your eyes. Let your feet rest evenly on the floor and let your hands lie quietly on your thighs. Now, imagine that you are standing up with your feet together. Then, gracefully (because in our imagination we can be graceful!), kneel down and pause, with your imaginary body kneeling quiet and still. Then, still in your imagination, put your hands on the ground in front of you and bow your imagined forehead to the ground. Do this several times. I often do it three times, in the name of God, Creator, Redeemer and Giver of Life.

Then continue quietly with your day or your usual spiritual practice.

# Chapter 6

# Help Me to Look Forward to Tomorrow

## Looking Forward Confidently

I have never really minded the prospect of growing older. One of my favourite authors as a young adult was the 20th century Anglican novelist Elizabeth Goudge. She is one of the few authors I have read who can convey the inner spiritual reality of being human convincingly. She also writes powerfully, not just about the inner lives of children but about the end of life and old age. And as a young woman, I wanted to become like some of her older characters when I grew older, women who had lived and loved and suffered and found wisdom. Women who had the gift of making people feel they mattered and were special. I wanted to be wise. I wanted to be of use to others. I didn't want to suffer, but somehow in my naive youth I managed to overlook the idea that wisdom and suffering do tend to be inextricably linked! With that as a goal, growing older seemed attractive rather than otherwise.

Now I have reached an age where I have experienced a little more of the usual human round of joy and sadness, and aches and pains remind me daily of my mortality. I find I am deeply thankful that I have encountered the Alexander technique and can use it to help navigate the very physical changes and challenges that accompany aging. I am also thankful to it for the daily discipline of letting go, of becoming quiet, which can help me with the deeper and wider challenges of letting go which belong to every aging human.

One reason for being able to look forward to tomorrow confidently is precisely the fact that help is available. I know that, whatever happens, the path on which I walk into the future is not one I need to walk alone. In addition to my personal practice of the Alexander technique there are my Alexander colleagues and teachers and students who teach and encourage and support me. Then there are other disciplines I can go to and learn from. I have been studying the work of Bonnie Bainbridge Cohen, a wise and profound teacher of bodily awareness. I can practise the gentler disciplines of Qi Gong and Tai Chi now that it seems wisest to let go of the more energetic art of Aikido I studied in my youth.

And the Christian tradition, as well as other faith traditions, teaches that we are not alone with our struggles, or our joys come to that. Recently I heard theologian, Sam Wells, vicar of St Martin-in-the-Fields, London, say that the whole point of the Incarnation and, indeed, of the cross within Christianity, is that God is with us. He proposes a theology of *being with*, of God being with us in Christ and us being with one another and with God.[79] So God, and others, are there to help, to be with us, to share in the suffering, to dance alongside us in the joys. And Francis prays *help me to…* throughout his prayer, confident that help is available from God, from the Love to which he gave his life.

One of the aspects of the Christian tradition that has become more meaningful for me in recent years, perhaps as a result of aging, is the communion of saints: the idea that we are surrounded and accompanied on our journey by the saints of every age. *Saint* can mean St Francis or St Clare, or another of my friends, St Werburgh. These are our official saints, so to speak, the saints that the 14th century mystic, Julian of Norwich, referred to as our 'kind neighbours'.[80]

Saints can also refer to our unknown, unnamed ancestors, the mothers and fathers of faith and courage and love to whom we owe our very existence. And it can mean those whom we have loved and who have loved us and are no longer here. All those saints are available to help me face tomorrow confidently, knowing I am not and can never be alone. This also means I don't have to make it up as I go along. I don't have to invent from scratch how to live my life well. I can learn from the wisdom of the past and lean on the faith of the past.

I find an arrogance in some modern thinking, a tendency to disparage the wisdom of the past, as if those who lived in earlier times were somehow stupid. I recognise it in myself, and work to notice when I fall into that habit of thinking. Because I don't think people in the past were less intelligent, insightful, or wise than in our present age, not at all.

There is a similar disparaging of oral societies by literate societies. I remember watching a programme about an indigenous people residing within the Amazon jungle. An adult member of this people would know the names, uses, seasonal appearance and growing places of hundreds of plants. I remember thinking then that this man was certainly no less intelligent than someone who would need to point a phone at a plant to identify it, or who would have to call a plumber to unblock a sink. The knowledge and wisdom of indigenous communities and earlier societies is not stupidity, but wisdom more technological societies have lost. So, I question whether my own sophisticated, clever, society is necessarily superior to what has gone before.

I do believe in progress. In many ways, much of the world is better today than it was in the past. There is less violence, less poverty than in earlier times; modern medicine is extraordinary, and just from the point of view of modern dentistry there is no time in which I would rather have been alive. But in other areas, other ways of knowing than the strictly scientific, I feel we have lost wisdom, lost knowledge. In areas of embodied knowing, spiritual knowing, the past had skills and wisdom that mainstream culture lacks today. If I practice humility, I can learn from the communion of saints that went before me, as indeed can anyone, whatever their religious beliefs.

So, I have recently been exploring, via the miracle of the internet, more traditional churches than my own. I have been *leaning* both on modern technology *and* ancient wisdom simultaneously, and enjoying the paradox of that. Specifically, I have been learning to pray the psalms. Christians, having received the gift of the psalms from our Jewish sisters, brothers and ancestors, have been praying them daily for two thousand years. I can think that this is old fashioned, boring and dry and dismiss it as not for me. Not modern enough, not radical enough. Or I can remain open and curious, and try it and see what happens. I can apply the Alexander technique and inhibit that first 'oh this is boring and old-fashioned and irrelevant to the modern world' thought and with gentle curiosity, by dipping my toes into the waters of praying the psalms.

What I am discovering or remembering, is that speech is a physical act. When I recite or sing a psalm the words enter my body, the oxygen goes deep into my lungs, it literally forms the bones within me that are growing and changing throughout my life. I can let the psalms, ancient songs of hope, anger, lament and exaltation, form my bones. I can notice how they make me feel more alive. Traditionally, there is a pause mid-way between the verse of the psalm, marked in Anglican service books by an asterisk (*). I once asked an elderly nun why they pause for a couple of seconds like this mid-verse and she replied, 'so we don't run out of breath'. Nothing romantic about nuns! So that is undoubtedly true. But I also find myself wondering, as an Alexander teacher, about that still point of silence mid-verse. A point where the breath enters the body.

The Alexander technique started life as a method of teaching breathing—the founder had breathing and voice problems during public speaking. But we don't really teach people how to breathe. Rather, we teach people to be quiet so that the breath does itself. As one of my teachers says, we are breathed more than we breathe.[81] From this perspective, that moment of silence mid-verse becomes, for me, 'the still point of the turning world'.[82]

It is a moment to experience the greater Silence within and behind all words and to let *It* breath *me*. And all of that richness was lying there quietly, waiting for me to discover it, once I had gained enough humility to be willing to learn from old-fashioned, boring Anglican worship, and once I was willing to take the time that it takes to experience it!

So, I have fellow travellers to give me confidence. A communion of saints to teach me and help me and keep me company. I don't have to do this alone. And — *and* this is a source not only of confidence, but of profound relief — I don't have to be perfect either. I don't even have to succeed. Our only greatness, Rohr says, is the one we share with the whole communion of saints; and we don't need to be correct, only connected'.[83] So my task is not to do it alone and brilliantly, but just to do what is given me to do day by day, and to keep in touch: to keep in touch with and be willing to lean on and learn from my wider Alexander community; to keep in touch with and learn from thinkers wiser and more learned than myself, with Francis and F M Alexander, with St Clare and Bonnie Bainbridge Cohen, with my parents and grandparents.

Returning to Elizabeth Goudge, she writes of one character who 'counselled simplicity, that day by day waiting upon the will of God, as revealed in the events which each day brought, as the only road to sanity'.[84] There is help available from both the living and the dead. When I lack faith and wisdom — which is often — I lean on the faith and wisdom of those more courageous, wiser, and closer to God than myself. And I ask them to help me to live well, and to learn to live simply and to wait upon God, day by day by day.

## Looking Forward Courageously

Fear is a normal human emotion. Those who are totally without fear are a danger to themselves and others. But fear is also one of the emotions that can lead us to close down, to tense up, to narrow in our views and our experiences, to harden our hearts, to stiffen our necks! And, like the stiff necks I talked about in an earlier chapter, fear is a spiritual as well as an emotional and physical reality. Perhaps it is that property of fear to close us down and harden our hearts that leads to the constant call of scripture, do not be afraid. Of course, if we were not afraid, we would not need to ask for help to look forward courageously because we only need courage when we are afraid. Indeed, without fear we would never learn how to be courageous at all because we only learn to be courageous by the practice of needing to *be* courageous!

One of the commonest human fears is the fear of death. Jesus Christ said almost nothing about what happens after death. There is the lovely, kind reassurance to the thief dying alongside him on the cross that later that afternoon they would be together in Paradise. There is the reference to His Father's house holding many mansions and that he was going there, ahead of his friends. But he also said that for a grain of wheat to bear fruit it had to fall into the ground and die. The kenotic path of letting go, of dying to self is, for me, at the very heart of Christ's teachings and of the teachings of Francis and Clare of Assisi, his followers.

Humans tend not to want to die. Physical life is what we know, and it gives us so much. Laughter and raindrops, sunshine and chocolate, the touch of a lover, the embrace of a child. And the unknown is scary. Death is an unknown country. But religious traditions have always encouraged seekers to face up to the reality of death regularly, even daily. Christianity is no exception.

Towards the end of his life Francis wrote an extra verse to his song of the creatures:

By Death our Sister, praised be,
From whom no-one alive can flee
Woe to the unprepared.
But blessed be those who do your will
And follow your commandments still.

I sing these words more or less every day. That means I am confronted, daily, by the invitation to remember my mortality and eventual death. This is not a morbid thing to do. It is to face reality. It is also a liberating act because it puts the often rather petty worries of my daily life into perspective. It invites me to notice, value and appreciate what really matters. The *woe* that is the condition of the *unprepared* is that, not accepting the reality of their death, it is easy for them to squander the time that they have, overlooking the ordinary miracle of being alive, the daily wonders and pleasures of our physical, embodied existence.

Daily meditation upon our mortality is a wisdom practice in the Franciscan tradition, because it means I get to know Death as my Sister. Not my enemy, not the ultimate failure, but my sister. There is a relief, a blessing, even in death. Francis added this verse because he saw death as another expression of the presence of God.[85]

A few years ago, there was a science fiction programme on the BBC called *Torchwood*. In one series it explored the idea that everyone, for some reason I now cannot remember, stopped dying. Nobody died. At first, that would seem wonderful. The programme subtly made the point that it was not wonderful at all. Suffering didn't end, only death. Eventually, people became desperate for a return to the natural cycle of life and death. Death is sad, and early, premature death can be tragic. But it is not the worst thing that can happen to a human. Like sleep at the end of a tiring but happy day, death can bless us, and Francis saw it as a blessing, as his kindly sister.

Singing the song of the creatures, with its verse about Sister Death is, for me, part of preparing to die gently, gladly, trustingly. The *letting go* of contemplative prayer and the Alexander technique is another such preparation. Each time I stop and notice that I am holding unnecessary tension in my legs and let it go I am preparing, in a tiny way, to let go of my physical existence. Each time I notice a thought chattering in my mind during prayer and let it go I am preparing myself to enter a Silence greater than my little self. Each time I notice my tendency to curl in upon myself and, instead, stop that movement and allow myself to gently open, I am preparing to open to the changes that death will bring me. Delio says that prayer is a deep relationship of 'God breathing in us' and that it requires change and conversion. 'And where there is change, there is the letting go of the old and the giving birth to the new. To pray is to be open to the new, to the future in God'.[86]

The Franciscan interpretation of the Resurrection is that there is nothing, simply nothing, out of which God cannot bring some good, and that includes my eventual death. I pray for courage because in common with most humans I *am* afraid of the unknown and death is the unknown country. But I also pray that, by the time I get there, the fear itself will have changed into a joyful expectancy. And I hope that my final letting go will be gentle and joyfully Franciscan!

# Embodied Prayer Practice: Singing a Psalm

The psalms, sometimes called the songbook of the Bible, allow us 'to read soul-deep into the life of some of our ancestors of faith'.[87]

Some of what we read is glorious, some of it is shocking, some of it tender and uplifting, other parts petty and spiteful. The psalms take the best and the worst of human nature and bring all of it before God in prayer. They are full of the usual human fears — and equally full of the reassuring call of the Divine not to be afraid. In the West we have formed the habit of silent reading. Scriptures were never meant for this kind of reading. They were meant to be utterances, physical acts that changed both those who uttered the words and those who heard them.

To *sing* a psalm is to allow it to enter even more deeply into your body. The words and the breath that you take to shape those words become part of your bones as you breathe deeply, and the oxygen feeds into each cell of your body. And that is one reason why we must not be uncritical of the words we sing. If we choose to sing the difficult psalms, the violent, hate-filled psalms as well as the glorious, comforting, uplifting psalms, then we need to sing them in acknowledgement that these words show the dark depths of human nature and bring them into the light of Love. They are not there as an example for us to follow but as words to respond to, and sometimes the response is one of anger and disagreement and rightly so.

If you are from a Christian or Jewish heritage you may already be familiar with the psalms and have favourite versions of favourite psalms. If they are unknown territory then see them as explorations by an ancient people of faith of what it means to be human, and what it means to be human in the light of the Divine. Find a short one, like 117, 134 or 150 to start with, or an uplifting one, like 8 or 19.

Singing a psalm is just a question of finding a note and starting. All on one note is fine. It really doesn't matter what you sound like. Part of what you are doing is exploring the feel of the words in your mouth and their sound in your ears. It is not a performance for others, it is for you and your body and your spiritual formation. And for God. Your version may have the asterisk (*) mid-verse that marks the breathing space, the pause. This is an opportunity for you to experience that 'still point of the turning world', a moment of utter silence, of waiting and letting go, of being breathed by the Divine.

Allow yourself to stand quietly and then sing a psalm. Explore the words and the stillness within the words. At the asterisk, Jim Cotter suggests that after saying a line out loud you imagine it echoing back to you as if from the other side of a valley.[88]

The words are prayer and so is the silence. And it is in the silence that you are learning to let go. You are preparing, in a tiny but important way, for the letting go into Sister Death that we must all do at last. You are embodying prayer.

# Chapter 7

# Befriending Ourselves

## Friends or Enemies? Body and Soul

Our bodies matter. Whether we are atheists who just want to live and move as easily and enjoyably as possible for as long as possible, or Christians or people of other faiths for whom the body is a gift from the Divine and a window *onto* the Divine, bodies matter. There are few people who would say otherwise. Yet, the general silence on the body's importance in European philosophy, theology and spiritual writing 'easily suggest that the body is something to be controlled not loved; ignored and overcome rather than cherished'.[89] Our secular culture West has not, I would say, made things much better. The body is still objectified rather than experienced, a source of shame or competition or a site of struggle rather than a gift to be nurtured, enjoyed, and delighted in.

One of the psalms in the Bible says, 'For it was you who formed my inward parts; you knit me together in my mother's womb. I praise you, for I am fearfully and wonderfully made' (Psalm 139: 13–14). At the heart of Franciscan spirituality is an appreciation for the wonder of creation. Alexander work is a tool for learning more about, sensing more accurately, and living more easily in my physical, spiritual, fleshy, emotional, whole created self. And the more clearly I see the part of creation that is *me*, the more I can appreciate, delight in, and revere the whole self that I have been given to enjoy; from there, the more clearly I will see, enjoy and revere the Creator in whose image I am created. So, Francis, Clare and Alexander encourage me to move away from a view of the body as somehow the enemy to a place where body and soul are friends.

There is a quote that is attributed to St Theresa of Avila that is pertinent to repeat here:

> Christ has no body now on earth but yours; no hands but yours; no feet but yours.
> Yours are the eyes through which the compassion of Christ must look out on the world.
> Yours are the feet with which He is to go about doing good.[89a]

The Christian faith makes the extraordinary claim that it is through me, through my physical, embodied, fleshy self that Christ, the Divine Incarnate One, now acts in the world, to bless, to comfort, to heal and to help suffering humanity. So why would I not revere, study, care for and love my body, if it is also Christ's body? And why would I not revere, study and care for each human body in the world, if in each person I meet I am also meeting Christ?

Franciscan spirituality is also a spirituality of simplicity. Simplicity of speech, of lifestyle and, for me, simplicity of movement. Alexander work, when I recollect it, helps me to move simply, quietly, easily, letting go of unnecessary effort and unneeded tension. It can help me, too, to look calmly at *how* I live and to consider how lightly I can walk on this planet, our Mother Earth.

And, as I have explored in this book, Alexander work helps me to ask for help when I need it, to physically lean on the ground God gives to support me, and to lean on the other humans She gives me too, both the living and the dead. It allows me to make space and quietness for those I meet and to meet them with joy and peace. It encourages me to look forward to tomorrow with confidence and courage, with hope that, as Julian of Norwich said, 'all will be well and all shall be well'.

## Friends or Enemies? Alexander and Clare

One of the things that attracted me to the Franciscan spiritual path was the presence of St Clare, Francis' friend and adviser, and her gentle spiritual wisdom. I find Christianity, along with the other major world faith traditions, still stubbornly patriarchal. The imagery and the language we use for the Divine is overwhelmingly male in many, and perhaps most, churches. For many, and again, perhaps most, people, the Divine, even the God they *don't* believe in, is male, white, and straight!

Though Francis himself honoured and recognised the value of the feminine and let himself—most unusually for a man of his time—be advised by a woman, the voice of St Clare in Franciscan studies and thought is only now really beginning to emerge. I see myself as a feminist, as being sensitive to the tendency to overlook or suppress the female voice which occurs in scripture, in history, in literature and film, and in many workplaces. So, I was surprised and saddened when I read the first draft of this book to realise that I, too, had unconsciously suppressed the voice of St Clare. She was nowhere to be seen, nowhere to be heard. I, like most women and men today, have internalised the tendency to overlook the female voice. I, therefore, went back and consciously made space for Clare, as I seek to make space for my students, so that she could expand and take up her own space.

While the equality of the sexes is closer in Europe than in some other parts of the world, it is still a long way off. The supposedly 'default' human is a white, cisgender man. This can be seen in medicine, where most drugs are tested on male bodies, not female ones. It can be seen in statuary, where the past and the present are overwhelmingly represented by statues of the bodies of white men. It can be seen in the study of anatomy, where the majority of anatomical representations and models are male, unless a specifically female process is being described.

Somatic disciplines, too, were largely developed by and for men, and the assumption is that cisgender men represent 'natural' or 'normal' ways of moving and standing. But movement and posture are not neutral, they are both cultural and gendered. And so is anatomy. Bonnie Bainbridge Cohen says that when she began studying anatomy in 1958, the bones of the pelvis were collectively called the *innominate* bone–the bone with no name. She linked this to the sexual attitudes prevailing at the time, noting how cultured and historical anatomy is.[90] I would add that it is also gendered. Different cultures walk differently, sit differently, and so do men and women who participate in those cultures.

Ingold points out the long-standing tendency in Western thought to elevate culture over the ground of nature and to be prone to what he calls 'the valorization of upright posture'.[91] That is a Western tendency, and it is also a patriarchal tendency. Women are associated with nature and with the ground, men with culture and the head!

I do not think the Alexander technique is immune from this unconscious male bias. I don't see how it could be since it was invented by a white Edwardian man. For example, Alexander said nothing, as far as I am aware, about the area of the pubic synthesis, the front of the pelvis, which is at least as important for easily integrated movement as the back of the pelvis. He was a product of his culture and time. He focused on the head, the neck and 'going up' —those male, civilised preoccupations. His classic directions go no lower than the knees, so neither the feet nor the ground, let alone the front of the pelvis, received much attention.

I see a need to critique the Alexander technique and our practice for its hidden male and, indeed, white, Eurocentric bias. Just as Clare provides a feminine balance to my Franciscan path, so too do I feel that Alexander work also needs to acknowledge and balance the influence of culture and gender.

I suspect that what we teach as *natural* movement in Alexander work can all too easily relate specifically to *male movement*. I, therefore, seek consciously to notice and undo that bias in my own learning, practice and teaching, as much as I can. For example, I have come to the conclusion that for many women, the freedom to broaden, to find the ground, and to find the power in their belly matters at least as much to their well-being, their confidence, their growth and their strength as the traditional Alexander focus on *lengthening* or *going up*. And in my own study, I now seek out teachers who can help me learn more about spirals and circles and spheres which help me relate with ease and freedom to my own embodied womanhood. I also look forward to learning from my trans and non-binary siblings how, as an Alexander teacher, I can help them find ease and comfort within their own beautiful bodies.

## Friends or Enemies? Alexander and Francis

Throughout my training, I was conscious of an ambivalence about the Alexander technique. It is powerful and beautiful. It can and does transform lives, relieves pain, enhances performance for dancers, musicians and actors, deepens embodied experience, and teaches a way of being present to myself and to each moment. I see its founder as someone with racist views whose writings can sometimes suggest that he thought he alone had discovered the secret of individual perfection and the perfection of the human race.

So, perhaps there is a contradiction between the Alexander technique and the Christian contemplative life? Martin Laird says that contemplation cannot be reduced to a technique. He argues that the word technique suggests a certain control that aims for a pre-determined outcome and that contemplative practice is not like that. It simply 'disposes us to allow something to take place'.[92]

If the Alexander technique must be all about conscious control, then perhaps there *is* a contradiction there. After all, one of Alexander's books is called *Constructive Conscious Control of the Individual*.[93] And if the Alexander technique is about the individual perfecting themselves and teachers helping students to become perfect, then I do see a contradiction, not just between Alexander and contemplation, but between Alexander and Christianity itself. And this possible contradiction may be why, in common with some other teachers, I find I prefer to refer to the Alexander *work*, rather than the Alexander *technique*.

However, I am far from being the first Christian to weave the Alexander technique into their life and work and prayer. The great 20th-century Archbishop William Temple was a student of Alexander and, at one time, before amplification in churches became common, it was well-known among clergy, who had Alexander lessons to overcome 'clergyman's throat'! Like George Bowden, and other Christians before us, I have come to see it as a spiritual discipline, one that can help me put 'Thy will be done' into practice in my daily life.

So, perhaps, if Laird's distinction is correct, the Alexander work can be *either* a technique *or* a practice. And perhaps what makes it one rather than the other is simply our intention and the spiritual or philosophical frame in which we locate it.

The Sufi teacher Kabir Helminski describes his early spiritual path when he learned to meditate, to work on himself and become more conscious and more present. He said that he noticed that meditation certainly helped him become more attentive and present, but not necessarily kinder or more forgiving. He even noticed a tendency in himself to become rather aloof and to see himself as somehow 'above' morality. He found Sufism to be the antidote he needed to the preoccupation with himself that his meditation seemed to foster.[94]

I suspect that any path of self-development, whether its starting point is spiritual or physical, has as its shadow side a tendency toward a preoccupation with self. The self becomes the goal, the only endpoint of the self-development work. I meditate (or study Alexander, practise yoga, or keep fit) for my own benefit and for my benefit alone. And this subtle and very human preoccupation can also be accompanied by a sense of superiority, over all those poor messy, unfit, chaotic humans out there who lack the discipline to meditate, practice yoga, keep fit etc. The skilful practitioner can, as Helminski noticed, begin to feel aloof from the mess and the muddle that is the reality of life for most humans.

Helminski found the antidote to a preoccupation with self in the path of love and service that is Sufism. My own chosen path of love and service is Christianity. And I think it is the *intention* to use the Alexander technique in the service of God and of suffering humanity—which includes myself—that moves it from technique to spiritual practice in my own life. What I teach and what I practise does not really change. What changes is the direction in which I travel, the ultimate goal and end of my life.

An Alexander teacher who is an atheist might find such a framework or direction in philosophy, humanism, education, socialism, or simply in the genuine desire to do good. Wherever it is found, the framework means that the end point of my work includes, yet goes beyond, myself. The endpoint is us—me *and* others, me *and* the world around me, me *and* the Kin-dom of Heaven.

I have said that what I teach and practise does not change if my focus is *us* rather than *me* alone. However, Alexander taught us the profound connection between ends and means, and Richard Rohr says that how we do anything is how we do everything. When the end point of my work is compassion and *Thy will be done*, then that goal will inevitably, and in spite of my failings and imperfections, permeate and colour all that I do and how I do everything.

Richard Rohr founded an organisation which is called the *Centre for Action and Contemplation*. He says that the most important word in the title is *and*. 'We need both compassionate action *and* contemplative practice for the spiritual journey. Without action, our spirituality becomes lifeless and bears no authentic fruit. Without contemplation, all our doing comes from ego, even if it looks selfless, and it can cause more harm than good'.[95]

The person who seeks to do good in the world without a spiritual practice can easily become consumed by anger, despair or self-righteousness. The contemplative whose practice never issues forth in compassionate action is missing the point of the contemplative life, which is love. Jesus commanded us to love God, one part of the contemplative life. And to love others as ourselves, is the other part of the contemplative life. As our love for God deepens, so does our compassion for the world. Contemplative prayer and spiritual practice both help us to soften the heart and turn us outward. They help us to live compassionately in the midst of the mess and the muddle of human life and all of creation, rather than seeking to somehow leave it all behind. As our compassion deepens so does our awareness of God, the Divine, Reality, the Sacred Other who is intimately linked to myself.

Karen Armstrong argues that, before the Enlightenment, religion was seen as a skill much more than as a set of beliefs. It was a practice, something people did. Its truths were discovered by constant, dedicated practise. You didn't accept the truths and then practice the religion. You practised the religion in order to understand and accept its truths. 'Religion is a practical discipline that teaches us to discover new capacities of mind and heart. Like any skill, religion requires perseverance, work and discipline. Religion can transform the smallest and most mundane of daily actions into a ritual that can make God present, and lead to an experience of God as a transcendent presence within'. [96]

I can only speak of my own tradition, but I feel that for too long Christianity has focused too much on what people should or shouldn't believe and too little on walking in the way of Jesus of Nazareth as a practice of love and compassion. As a result, people think that, unless they accept every word of the Bible as literally true (and many Christians, myself included, don't), then the Christian tradition has nothing to offer them in terms of how they live their lives, how they navigate the deep struggles of being human, how they love or how they die.

As Alexander taught, you first need to recognise a habit in order to change it. The over-focus on intellectual belief and the lack of teaching about practice is one habit that, for me, Christians need first to see—and then to change. We have too often made religious belief a barrier to people finding God. I think the time may now be right to redress that balance and both Alexander and Francis have things to offer to this rebalancing.

Some people use the Alexander technique to play the violin or to sing more easily. Others learn it in order to run without injury. Many people come to it to find relief from chronic pain. It is a technique, or a practice, that helps you to do the things you do with ease and grace and pleasure. I use it to practise my religion, to pray, and to follow Jesus Christ in the footsteps of Francis and Clare.

I turn to Alexander and Francis and Clare for help as I do my best to do my little bit in building the kin-dom of heaven. To live love in the world. I am grateful for their help.

# Embodied Prayer Practice: Centering Prayer

Martin Laird says that contemplation, or the life of stillness, is not the opposite of the active life. The opposite of the contemplative life is, rather, the reactive life. He writes about the 'highly habituated emotional styles and lifestyles that keep us constantly reacting to life like victimizing victims, ever more convinced that the videos that dominate and shape our awareness are in fact true. The life of stillness gradually heals this split and leads us into wide-open fields where buried treasure lies (Mt 13.45–46)'.[97]

I practise a kind of contemplation called 'Centering Prayer' as taught by Cynthia Bougeault in her book *Centering Prayer and Inner Awakening*, who in turn learned it from the American monk, Thomas Keating. It is really very simple.

You sit in a chair with your back supported in a gently upright position, both feet on the floor. Or you kneel on a prayer stool. You choose a 'sacred word'. It can be a spiritual word, like 'God', or 'Jesus', or 'the Divine'. The Jesus Prayer is an ancient practice of repeating the name of Christ with each breath. Alternatively, the word can be more neutral, like Peace or Love. Or it can be a very short phrase like 'Be still' or 'Let go'.

You start to repeat the word or short phrase as you enter a time of quiet. At some point, you let go of the word or phrase. When thoughts come, and they will come, you notice and return to repeating the sacred word. Then you let it go again.

You remain for a period of time. If you have never done this before then try 10 minutes. Gradually increase this to 20 to 25 minutes. Ideally do it twice a day. That's it. You don't expect anything and you don't judge the experience. There is no right or wrong, no good or bad. You just turn up, stay for as long as you intended and do it regularly. What happens is the work of silence and, as Cynthia Bourgeault says, it is no one's business, not even your own; it is between your innermost being and God.[98]

Each time you notice a thought, let it go. Each time you notice you are trying too hard, stop. Remember, you are just sitting. Each time you notice you are holding yourself up, let go and trust the support beneath you. Practised over a lifetime this simple work of silence will change who you understand yourself to be, how you live, and what and how you believe.

## Chapter 8

# Final Words from Clare and Francis

St Clare spoke these words on her death bed, addressing her own soul. I would like to address them to you:

> 'Go forth now, you have a good escort. The one who created you has provided for you.
> The one who created you will guard you as a mother does her little child.'[99]

And adapting St Francis:

> Live today quietly, easily.
> Lean on the ground, on reality, and on those who support you trustfully, restfully.
> Wait for the unfolding of what will be, patiently and serenely.
> Open your heart to all that is, joyfully, peacefully.
> Look forward to tomorrow confidently, courageously.

And remember, help is always available.

# Author Biography

Jennifer is a member of the Third Order of the Society of St Francis, a teacher of the Alexander technique and an ordained minister in the Church of England. She has a PhD in well-being in education, holds qualifications in teaching and counselling and has worked in education for over 30 years. She is the creator of Celebrating Strengths, a spiritual and emotional well-being project used by schools in the UK and abroad. She is the author of numerous books, articles and resources for schools and has been translated into Italian and Danish. Her full list of publications can be found at **www.jennyfoxeades.com**.

She has studied a variety of martial arts and sees bread making as a much neglected spiritual pathway. She lives in Macclesfield, Cheshire with her sourdough starter, Ethel, and other family members.

# Previous Books

*Classroom Tales: Using Storytelling to Build Emotional,*
*Social and Academic Skills across the Primary Curriculum*
Published by Jessica Kingsley, London
ISBN-13: 978-1-84310-304-2 and ISBN-10: 1-84310-304-4

*Celebrating Strengths: Building Strengths-based Schools*
Published by CAPP Press
ISBN: 978-1-906366-01-8 and ISBN: 978-1-906366-02-5

# References

1.  Dewey, J., 1922. Human nature and conduct. 2012 ed. Online Publisher: Digireads.com Publishing, p. 13

2.  TSSF, 2020. Third Order Society of St Francis European Province. Available at: https://tssf.org.uk/about-the-third-order/the-principles-of-the-third-order/

3.  Schmalzl, L., Crane-Godreua, M. A. & Payne, P., 2014. Movement-based embodied contemplative practices. Frontiers in Human Neuroscience, Volume 8, p. 1

4.  Rohr, R., 2020. *Joy and Sadness: A Lesson from Merton's Hermitage.* Available at: https://cac.org/daily-meditations/joy-and-sadness-a-lesson-from-mertons-hermitage-2020-11-22

5.  Rohr, R., 2020. *Between Two Worlds.* Available at: https://cac.org/daily-meditations/between-two-worlds-2020-04-26/

6.  Shusterman, R., 2008. Body Consciousness: A Philosophy of Mindfulness and Somaesthetics. Cambridge: Cambridge University Press

7.  Gooder, P., 2016. Body: Biblical Spirituality for the Whole Person. London: SPCK

8.  Bourgeault, C., 2003. The Wisdom Way of Knowing: Reclaiming an Ancient Tradition to Awaken the Heart. San Francisco: Jossey-Bass, p 28

9.  Fertman, B., 2018. Teaching by Hand, Learning by Heart. London: Mouritz, p. 36

10. Bainbridge Cohen, B., 2012. Sensing, Feeling, and Action: The Experiential Anatomy of Body-Mind Centering. Third ed. Northampton, USA: Contact Editions, p. 1

11. ibid., p. 5

12. Dewey, J., 1923. Introduction to F.M. Alexander's Constructive Conscious Control of the Individual. 1987 ed. Reading: Methuen, p. xiii

13. Spearing, E., 1998. Translator's Note. In: Revelations of Divine Love. Penguin Classics ed. s.l.:Penguin, p. xli

14. Peck, S., 1990. The Road Less Travelled. New Edition ed. s.l.: Arrow

15. Saint Francis of Assisi Quotes. Available at: https://www.quotes.net/quote/42579

16. Robb, F., 1999. Not to 'Do': An account of lessons in the Alexander Technique with Margaret Goldie. London: Camon Press, p. 81

17. Rohr, R., 2020. *The Second Conversion*. Available at: https://cac.org/daily-meditations/the-second-conversion-2020-05-26

18. TSSF, 2020. Third Order Society of St Francis European Province. Available at: https://tssf.org.uk

19. Rohr, R., 2014. Eager to Love: The Alternative Way of Francis of Assisi. London: Hodder & Stoughton, p. 114

20. Fertman, B., 2018. Teaching by Hand, Learning by Heart. London: Mouritz, p. xvii

21. Laird, M., 2011. A Sunlit Absence: Silence, Awareness, and Contemplation. Oxford: OUP, p.37

22. Rohr, R., 2014. Eager to Love: The Alternative Way of Francis of Assisi. London: Hodder & Stoughton, p. 101

23. ibid., p. 101

24. The Rule of St Clare, 1982. Francis and Clare, The Complete Works. The Classics of Western Spirituality ed. New York: Paulist Press, p. 219

25. Laird, M., 2011. A Sunlit Absence: Silence, Awareness, and Contemplation. Oxford: OUP

26. Rohr, R., 2020. *Community as Alternative Consciousness*. Available at: https://cac.org/daily-meditations/community-as-alternative-consciousness-2020-06-01/

27. Bourgeault, C., 2003. The Wisdom Way of Knowing: Reclaiming an Ancient Tradition to Awaken the Heart. San Francisco: Jossey-Bass, p 31

28. Schaffner, A. K., 2016. Exhaustion: A History. Columbia: Columbia University Press

29. ibid., p.134

30. Wells, S., 2020. Online 'Great Sacred Music' https://www.stmartin-in-the-fields.org/

31. Brueggeman, W., 2014, 2017. Sabbath as Resistance: Saying No to the Culture of Now. New Edition with Study Guide ed. Louisville, Kentucky: Westminster John Knox Press

32. Peterson, C. & Seligman, M. E. P., 2004. Character strengths and virtues: A classification and handbook. Washington DC: American Psychological Association.

33. Rohr, R., 2014. Eager to Love: The Alternative Way of Francis of Assisi. London: Hodder & Stoughton, p. 92

34. Sandberg, S., 2013. Lean In: Women, Work, and the Will to Lead. s.l.: W H Allen

35. Rohr, R., 2020. *Passing Over to Life*. Available at: https://cac.org/daily-meditations/lesson-four-passing-over-to-life-2020-04-09/

36. Dewey, J., 1922. Human nature and conduct. 2012 ed. Online Publisher: Digireads.com Publishing, p. 15

37. Norwich, J. o., 1980. Enfolded in Love: Daily Readings with Julian of Norwich. 2004 Enfolded in Love Series ed. s.l.: Darton, Longman & Todd, p. 13

38. Rohr, R., 2014. Eager to Love: The Alternative Way of Francis of Assisi. London: Hodder & Stoughton, p. 138

39. Gelb, M., 1987. Body Learning: An Introduction to the Alexander Technique. Avon: Aurum Press, p. 68, (my italics)

40. Dewey, J., 1916. Democracy and Education. 2011 Simon ed. s.l.: Simon & Brown, p. 14

41. Weil, S., 1959. Reflections on the right use of school studies with a view to the love of God. [Online] p. 3

42. Dewey, J., 1916. Democracy and Education. 2011 Simon ed. s.l.: Simon & Brown, p. 9

43. Rohr, R., 2014. Eager to Love: The Alternative Way of Francis of Assisi. London: Hodder & Stoughton, p. 178

44. Alexander, F. M., 1941. The Universal Constant in Living. 1986 ed. Long Beach: Centerline Press, p. 30

45. Alexander, F. M., 1910. Man's Supreme Inheritance. Forgotten Books, Classic Reprint Series ed. New York: Paul R Reynolds, p. 97

46. Fertman, B., 2018. Teaching by Hand, Learning by Heart. London: Mouritz, p. 21

47. ibid., p. 97

48. Bourgeault, C., 2003. The Wisdom Way of Knowing: Reclaiming an Ancient Tradition to Awaken the Heart. San Francisco: Jossey-Bass, p 75

49. McKay, A., 2020. What is conflict doing in God's world?. franciscan, 32(3), pp. 3-4.

50. Rohr, R., 2020. *The Gift of a Simple Life*. Available at: https://cac.org/daily-meditations/the-gift-of-a-simple-life-2020-10-08/

51. Armstrong, K., 2009. The Case For God: What Religion Really Means. London: The Bodley Head, p. 102

52. Bourgeault, C., 2008. The Wisdom Jesus: Transforming Heart and Mind - a New Perspective on Christ and His Message. Boulder: Shambala

53. Pierce Jones, F., 1997. Freedom to Change. New Edition ed. on-line: Mouritz, p. 97

54. TSSF, 2020. Third Order Society of St Francis European Province. Available at: https://tssf.org.uk/about-the-third-order/the-principles-of-the-third-order/

55. Rohr, R., 2014. Eager to Love: The Alternative Way of Francis of Assisi. London: Hodder & Stoughton, p. 172

56. Rohr, R., 2019. *Waiting and Unknowing*. Available at: https://cac.org/daily-meditations/waiting-and-unknowing-2019-12-01/

57. Rohr, R., 2020. *Loving God by Loving the World*. Available at: https://cac.org/daily-meditations/loving-god-by-loving-the-world-2020-05-21/

58. Fox Eades, J. M., 2008. Celebrating Strengths: Building Strengths-based Schools. Coventry: CAPP Press

59. Peterson, C. & Seligman, M. E. P., 2004. Character strengths and virtues: A classification and handbook. Washington DC: American Psychological Association.

60. Higgins, C., 2010. Working Conditions: The Practice of Teaching and the Institution of School. Journal of Philosophy of Education, 44(2-3), pp. 337-369.

61. Helminski, K., 1982, 2017. Living Presence: The Sufi Path to Mindfulness and the Essential Self. Revised ed. New York: Tarcher Perigee

62. ibid., p. 64

63. Ross, M., 2014. Silence: A User's Guide. London: Darton, Longman & Todd

64. Steindl-Rast, D., 2020. Good Reads. Available at: https://www.goodreads.com/quotes/557873-try-pausing-right-before-and-right-after-undertaking-a-new/

65. Kleinman, J., 2018. Alexander in Secondary and Tertiary Education. Self published: The Developing Self. p. 37

66. Kingsley, N., 2011. Free Yourself from Back Pain: A guide to the Alexander Technique. London: Kyle Cathie Limited, p. 73

67. Norwich, J. o., 1980. Enfolded in Love: Daily Readings with Julian of Norwich. 2004 Enfolded in Love Series ed. s.l.: Darton, Longman & Todd

68. McKibben, B., 2019. Falter: Has the Human Game Begun to Play Itself Out?. s.l. Wildfire, p. 255-6

69. Murray, T., 2020. Stillness, opportunity and the local church during the pandemic. Available at: https://www.psephizo.com/life-ministry/stillness-opportunity-and-the-local-church-during-the-pandemic

70. Herrigel, E., 1953. Zen in the Art of Archery: Training the Mind and Body to Become One. 1988 ed. London: Penguin
71. Bowden, G. C., 1965. F. Matthias Alexander and the Creative Advance of the Individual. London: L N Fowler & Co. Ltd, p. 22
72. ibid., p. 41
73. ibid., p. 20
74. Bourgeault, C., 2008. The Wisdom Jesus: Transforming Heart and Mind - a New Perspective on Christ and His Message. Boulder: Shambala
75. Bourgeault, C., 2003. The Wisdom Way of Knowing: Reclaiming an Ancient Tradition to Awaken the Heart. San Francisco: Jossey-Bass
76. ibid., p. 111
77. Schneider, M., 2012, 2016. Vision for Life: 10 Steps to Natural Eyesight Improvement. Revised ed. Berkeley: North Atlantic Books
78. Bourgeault, C., 2003. The Wisdom Way of Knowing: Reclaiming an Ancient Tradition to Awaken the Heart. San Francisco: Jossey-Bass
79. Wells, S., 2016. Hanging by a Thread: The Questions of the Cross. Norwich: Canterbury Press
80. Winkett, L., 2020. Heaven is a Noisy Place. Available at: https://www.bbc.co.uk/programmes/m000mbpf
81. Fertman, B., 2020. Grace of Sense. Available at: https://www.graceofsense.com/what-grace-of-sense-is-really-about/
82. Eliot, T., 1944. Four Quartets. 1959 ed. London: Faber, p. 15
83. Rohr, R., 2014. Eager to Love: The Alternative Way of Francis of Assisi. London: Hodder & Stoughton, p. 14
84. Goudge, E., 1958. The White Witch. London: Hodder & Stoughton, p. 357

   Greetham, B., 2006. Philosophy. Foundations ed. Basingstoke: Palgrave

85.  Cocksedge, S., 2010. Francis of Assisi, Living Prayer Today. Cambridge: Grove Books, p. 11

86.  Delio, I., 2004. Franciscan Prayer, s.l.: Franciscan Media, p. 28

87.  Cotter, J., 2006. Out of the Silence...Into the Silence. Harlech: Cairns Publications, p. xxiii

88.  ibid., p. xlii

89.  Gooder, P., 2016. Body: Biblical Spirituality for the Whole Person. London: SPCK

89a. https://catholic-link.org/quotes/st-teresa-of-avila-quote-christ-has-no-body-but-yours/

90.  Bainbridge Cohen, B., 2020. Free the Vital Energy and Illuminating Presence of Your Spine: A Body-Mind Centering Approach®, s.l.: s.n.

91.  Ingold, T., 2004. Culture on the Ground: The World Perceived Through the Feet. Journal of Material Culture, 9(3), p. 315

92.  Laird, M., 2006. Into the Silent Land. London: Darton, Longman and Todd Ltd

93.  Alexander, F. M., 1923. Constructive Conscious Control of the Individual. 1992 ed. London: Victor Gollancz Ltd.

94.  Helminski, K., 1982, 2017. Living Presence: The Sufi Path to Mindfulness and the Essential Self. Revised ed. New York: Tarcher Perigee, p. 54

95.  Rohr, R., 2020. *Our Foundational Commitment*. Available at: https://cac.org/daily-meditations/our-foundational-commitment-2020-01-05/

96.  Armstrong, K., 2009. The Case For God: What Religion Really Means. London: The Bodley Head, p. 4

97.  Laird, M., 2011. A Sunlit Absence: Silence, Awareness, and Contemplation. Oxford: OUP, p. 42

98.  Bourgeault, C., 2004. Centering Prayer and Inner Awakening. Plymouth: Cowley Publications, p. 6

99.  Rohr, R., 2014. Eager to Love: The Alternative Way of Francis of Assisi. London: Hodder & Stoughton, p. 151

# Further Reading

## Websites

https://alexandertechnique.com A good place to start with links to lots of resources

https://alexandertechnique.co.uk The website of the largest professional Alexander organisation in the UK

https://www.alexandertechniquebristol.co.uk/ An excellent site for the latest scientific research on the Alexander technique

https://tssf.org.uk/ The website of the Third Order of the Society of St Francis in the UK

https://cac.org The Centre for Action and Contemplation – a wealth of resources and teaching on the spiritual life

## Books

*F. Matthias Alexander: The Man and His Work* by Lulie Westfeldt 1998 (Mouritz) I think this is a great introduction but there are many books out there

I am also a fan of my teacher's book

*Teaching by Hand, Learning by Heart* by Bruce Fertman 2018 (Mouritz)

# Glossary of Terms

## Spiritual Terms

Centering prayer: a form of contemplative prayer which is traced back to the author of the Cloud of Unknowing (Anonymous, 1946) and was revived in the 20th century by Father Thomas Keating.

Contemplation: a 'long loving look at the Real' (Rohr), the prayer of silence; an essentially wordless prayer where thoughts are not followed, but are noticed and allowed to fall away, leaving an objectless awareness.

Dualism: the idea that there is a split between mind and body or spirit and matter. Often credited to René Descartes (1596–1650) but implicit in other philosophical and theological ideas as far back as Plato (427–347 BC).

False self: a term used in spiritual writings to refer to the part of the self that needs to get its own way and sees the world as separate. Other writers say there is no 'false' self to be removed, though we need to learn to see Reality and ourselves in union with Reality.

Friar: literally, 'little brother'. A term used for Franciscan monks. Part of the egalitarian nature of Franciscanism is that their community leaders are never called 'Father' or 'Mother', they are all brothers or sisters.

Grace: In Christian theology, grace is the undeserved, unearned gift of salvation, of the love of God.

Incarnation: a term used in theology to refer to God becoming human in Jesus Christ.

Kenosis (kenotic): Self-emptying. Theologically, used to refer to how God empties Herself to become human in Jesus Christ.

Kingdom of Heaven: Jesus often refers to the 'kingdom of heaven' (though some have argued it might better be translated as the 'republic' of heaven). He variously said it was 'close at hand' or 'within you'. It is a mysterious teaching. My interpretation is that it refers, not to a future time after death, but to a vision of a more equal, kinder, more compassionate world that is possible, that is coming, and that people of faith are called on to create. It is both here, now and not here yet!

Meditation: sometimes used interchangeably with contemplation but my understanding is that meditation has an object, like a prayer word or the breath whereas contemplation is objectless.

Providence: God, the work of God or the Divine in the world, the protective care of God or of nature as a spiritual power.

Sin: curving in on oneself; the illusion that we are separate from God and the rest of creation – and the actions that result from that illusion.

TSSF: The Third Order of the Society of St Francis, or tertiaries. A community of lay and ordained, married and single people following a rule of life they design for themselves, with a shared commitment to live simply, to work for social justice and to share the love of God.

## Alexander Terms

Direction: A way of restoring the body to balance or poise through thinking rather than through direct muscular effort. Direction can be verbal. Alexander's classic verbal directions are 'let the neck be free so that the head can go forward and up to allow the back to lengthen and widen and the knees to go forward and away'. However, for some people, visualising space or light or movement in the body can be more effective.

Faulty (Unreliable) sensory perception: a term used in the Alexander technique to refer to the fact that our senses—our perceptions—are not always reliable.

Inhibition: a deep, profound, neurological stopping or quiet; a pause before and after action.

Non-doing: allowing movement to happen; a very quiet, thoughtful movement with just the appropriate amount of tension.

Primary control: integrated movement, mind and body working in unity, moving and thinking as a whole, not as a collection of parts.

Semi-supine: I call this 'Coming to Quiet' and describe it in Embodied Prayer Practice 3 at the end of Chapter 2. It is a way of lying down and resting with eyes open, while staying fully awake and aware.

Use, good or bad: Alexander spoke about the 'use' of the self and used words like 'good' and 'bad' to describe how people move, stand, breathe and hold themselves. It's not a word I use myself as I always wonder who is using whom? But broadly, 'good use' is poise, integrated, easy movement; 'bad' use is when we use more tension than we need for an action or are unbalanced.

CHRISTIAN ALTERNATIVE
BOOKS

## THE NEW OPEN SPACES

Throughout the two thousand years of Christian tradition
there have been, and still are, groups and individuals
that exist in the margins and upon the edge of faith. But
in Christianity's contrapuntal history it has often been
these outcasts and pioneers that have forged contemporary
orthodoxy out of former radicalism as belief evolves to engage
with and encompass the ever-changing social and scientific
realities. Real faith lies not in the comfortable certainties of
the Orthodox, but somewhere in a half-glimpsed hinterland
on the dirt track to Emmaus, where the Death of God meets
the Resurrection, where the supernatural Christ meets the
historical Jesus, and where the revolution liberates
both the oppressed and the oppressors.

Welcome to Christian Alternative... a space at the
edge where the light shines through.
If you have enjoyed this book, why not tell other readers
by posting a review on your preferred book site.

# Recent bestsellers from Christian Alternative are:

## Bread Not Stones
The Autobiography of An Eventful
Life Una Kroll
The spiritual autobiography of a truly remarkable
woman and a history of the struggle for ordination in the
Church of England.
Paperback: 978-1-78279-804-0 ebook: 978-1-78279-805-7

## The Quaker Way
A Rediscovery
Rex Ambler
Although fairly well known, Quakerism is not well
understood. The purpose of this book is to explain how
Quakerism works as a spiritual practice.
Paperback: 978-1-78099-657-8 ebook: 978-1-78099-658-5

## Blue Sky God
The Evolution of Science and Christianity
Don MacGregor
Quantum consciousness, morphic fields and blue-sky
thinking about God and Jesus the Christ.
Paperback: 978-1-84694-937-1 ebook: 978-1-84694-938-8

## Celtic Wheel of the Year
Tess Ward
An original and inspiring selection of prayers combining
Christian and Celtic Pagan traditions, and interweaving
their calendars into a single pattern of prayer for
every morning and night of the year.
Paperback: 978-1-90504-795-6

### Christian Atheist
Belonging without Believing
Brian Mountford
Christian Atheists don't believe in God but miss him:
especially the transcendent beauty of his music,
language, ethics, and community.
Paperback: 978-1-84694-439-0 ebook: 978-1-84694-929-6

### Compassion Or Apocalypse?
A Comprehensible Guide to the Thoughts of
René Girard James Warren
How René Girard changes the way we think about
God and the Bible, and its relevance for our
apocalypse-threatened world.
Paperback: 978-1-78279-073-0 ebook: 978-1-78279-072-3

### Diary Of A Gay Priest
The Tightrope Walker
Rev. Dr. Malcolm Johnson
Full of anecdotes and amusing stories, but the Church
is still a dangerous place for a gay priest.
Paperback: 978-1-78279-002-0 ebook: 978-1-78099-999-9

Readers of ebooks can buy or view any of these bestsellers by
clicking on the live link in the title. Most titles are published in
paperback and as an ebook. Paperbacks are available
in traditional bookshops. Both print and ebook
formats are available online.

Find more titles and sign up to our readers' newsletter at
www.collectiveinkbooks.com/christianity Follow us on
Facebook at https://www.facebook.com/ChristianAlternative